Crisis in the East European Economy

The Spread of the Polish Disease

Edited by Jan Drewnowski

CROOM HELM   London & Canberra

ST. MARTIN'S PRESS   New York

© 1982 Jan Drewnowski
Croom Helm Ltd, Provident House, Burrell Row,
Beckenham, Kent BR3 1AT

British Library Cataloguing in Publication Data

Crisis in the East European Economy
   1. Europe, Eastern − Economic conditions
   I. Drewnowski, Jan
   330.9'47   HC244

   ISBN 0-7099-0826-1

First published in the United States of America in 1982

Library of Congress Cataloging in Publication Data
Main entry under title:

Crisis in the East European economy.

   Includes index.
   1. Europe, Eastern − Economic conditions − 1945 − Addresses,
essays, lectures. 2. Europe, Eastern − Economic policy − Addresses,
essays, lectures.
I. Drewnowski, Jan F.
HC244.C74   1982   330.947   82-42560
ISBN 0-312-17314-8

Typeset by Mayhew Typesetting, Bristol
Printed and bound in Great Britain

CONTENTS

INTRODUCTION: ZERO GROWTH, AND THE INTERNATIONAL NATURE OF THE POLISH DISEASE

Peter Wiles

2205447

There is a spectre haunting Eastern Europe: the spectre of zero growth. This is not the position of Poland since August 1980, when growth has been heavily negative. The 'Polish Disease' of our title is that general state of society that obtained in 1978–80, before the rise of Solidarity. Solidarity was a failed cure for the disease, and will surely have no parallel in other Communist countries.

Zero growth is, as the British have discovered, livable at personal level, though very uncomfortable and undesirable. Indeed it still leaves an excellent chance to everyone who is young or skilled or energetic to better himself substantially while others decline. But the British have no ideology of indefinite and internationally superior growth. A Marxist–Leninist on the other hand is wounded in that most sensitive portion of his anatomy, his religion.

We return to Britain later. But the Communist failure is unexplained: so the spectre haunts the students of Eastern Europe too. In the absence of either a plausible or a complete answer it is a privilege to have been asked by the editor to bring the debate into at least some sort of order.

We begin with economically orthodox explanations that are clearly invalid. Thus it has been said that the low recent performance is due to:

(1) The 1973 oil shock, which eventually penetrated the CMEA in 1978 when USSR, abandoning her original generosity, revised her prices. But USSR benefited from that act! And she benefits from the gold price too. Nor did Poland really suffer, since she was a big coal exporter, and the coal price did not lag far behind the oil price. Moreover on Western markets both countries' exports had kept pace with the dollar price from the first. As a group, then, these countries neither gained nor lost. Yet each individually is suffering.

(2) The exhaustion of labour reserves. The idea is that one generally adds more to national product by spending one rouble on putting the unemployed to work with an old and rather labour-intensive technology than by spending it on improving the technical equipment of a constant labour force. This seems to be true,[1] and it is indeed one of

the reasons why some countries in the middle ranks of international wealth comparison make very fast progress; they are able either to import sophisticated technology for a few or to provide a great volume of the simpler domestic type for many. But in our seven countries there has been such a reserve of labour since the early 1970s only in Poland, Bulgaria and Romania. So while the comparatively good performance of Bulgaria is thus easily accounted for the declining performance of the other six since 1975 is not, and Poland's and Romania's quite particularly not. These two have performed, not badly in an average way, but worst.

(3) The heavy defence burden, the irrational price system, the extraordinarily long lead times in investment, the unpopularity of collectivised agriculture, the unwieldy because overcentralised administration of everything, and especially of foreign trade . . . But all these drawbacks have plagued the system since its beginning, and it has performed excellently despite them in the past, thereby establishing beyond doubt some other virtue or virtues that outweighed them. Nothing indicates that any of these drawbacks have grown worse, quite the contrary. Thus computers have multiplied, the economics profession has been liberalised, wholesale prices have been sensibly reformed, formal investment criteria have had profitability built into them and managerial bonuses have been made dependent on profit. All these things argue weakly for more rational prices, and a greater influence of prices over allocation. Many co-operation agreements have been signed by Communist and foreign firms, thus cutting out the Ministries of Foreign Trade. In some countries the collective farms have been internally decentralised, in most more illegal economic activity is tolerated within them.

Let us pass over the various other drawbacks, frequently alleged that do not even exist. I mean notably the lack of incentives (cf. Drewnowski here, p. 74). Here are some economically orthodox suggestions that cannot be so easily dismissed, since they describe new difficulties:

(a) Diminishing returns to extractive industry, including agriculture. Returns diminish, of course, over time: there used to be better new fields to occupy than there now are. Moreover everybody knows where the best fields for agriculture lie, and they are indeed the ones first occupied, so this situation cannot be reversed. But this does not necessarily apply to mining and drilling. Nobody really knows what is in the ground, and it simply happens to be the case that recently

Romania has discovered nothing, Poland nothing good, and USSR only the Urengoy gas field. This latter is a find indeed, and will make a big difference, but the Soviet oil industry is in real trouble, with coal little better. However oil investment is a very small part of all Soviet invest- ment, and it is agriculture's claim that is cripplingly high (see Wiles here).

(b) The gradual accumulation of cash in the hands of the population. So long as the total stability of retail prices was an obsession ranking almost as part of the ideology of Marxism–Leninism, the very success of the system threatened suppressed inflation, since people becoming richer will save, and their accumulations can only find an outlet in buying something, but are virtually certain to grow faster than the supply of goods.[2] But suppressed inflation means longer queues, and so loss of time. And much of this time will be stolen from the work- place in long lunch hours, absenteeism etc. (Wiles, 1982). However queueing time stolen from one's employer cannot be very big. Thus if another half-hour a week was diverted in this way it would only lower hours worked by 1 per cent. Nevertheless there are large 'imponderable' issues here (see below).

(c) They have reached their minimum technological lag.[3] By a well- known simple paradox, a country's growth is enhanced by its being moderately backward. There is more to be learned, so progress can be more rapid. But one must be rich enough to buy the relevant proto- types, licences or education. It is, then, the middle-class nations that grow quickest, and our seven countries have been middle-class since Communism got them (except East Germany and the Czech lands).

Now, the assumption has hitherto been that nations will all even- tually import all the technology there is and catch up with the world leader (at present the USA, perhaps tomorrow West Germany or Japan). For this they need only time, reasonable public aid for the poorest, and borrowing for the rest. Thereafter no nation can grow faster than the rate permitted by the growth of world technological knowledge. But the Soviet-type economies have always stood somewhat apart from this assumption, since: (i) their research is exceedingly inefficient and they contribute little to world knowledge despite vast expenditures (this is because the KGB imposes obstacles to the foreign communication upon which research rests, and the rigid system of production hinders the manufacture of prototypes); and (ii) their capacity to develop their own research operationally, or to assimilate other people's research, is disgracefully low (this is because managerial bonus functions are incorrectly specified, and the new supply links that innovation requires are inordinately difficult to establish in a top-heavy, non-market hierarchical system; also the KGB and the Ministry of Foreign Trade are both jealous of economic intimacy with foreigners, so that the practical minor know-how cannot come in).

We have not space here to expand on these all-important and long-standing flaws.[4] But science and technology have now become so complicated that their assimilation is virtually a research project in itself. If your R & D system is fundamentally bad you will take so long to assimilate the last advance that you will not be able to assimilate the present one at all and will lose all its advantages, but must wait for the next one — and you will be late with it! This did not impede catching-up while you were really backward, but the Soviet-type economies may never catch up completely, and their present lag may be as short as it ever will be. Therefore they are already advancing only at the rate of world technological knowledge.

My own predilection is to examine what are ordinarily called the imponderables — a curious word, since none of the orthodox economic variables we have examined above can in fact be quantified in itself, let alone assigned a numerical effect. However they are in one way or another more formal and orthodox, more quantifiable in principle, more solidly based upon a logical 'homo economicus', than what follows. This does not subtract from, nor yet does it add to, the validity of the 'imponderables'. What could diminish their validity is their inaccurate or illogical handling; and this I must painfully avoid. Granted that all plausible explanations, coming from whatever body of thought, must be given a fair hearing. We have no reason to suppose that 'homo' is 'economicus'.

An economic system consists of human beings. If they have no confidence in it, and it makes them unhappy, they will not work well, and then the system will not function well. The workers will be both slow and careless, the planners will be cynical, irresponsible and uncritical. Not only goods and money, but also paid time, will be stolen from places of work. There will be embezzlement in high places. The trouble with 'homo economicus' is that he has no labour morale, let alone fluctuations in labour morale. Yet anyone who has ever worked in any organisation — or by himself — knows that labour morale is the most important factor of production.

Some of these results of low labour morale can have other causes. We have seen that suppressed inflation is itself a venial sin on a planner's part, if he is responsible at all; and that it too causes black markets and the theft of time. And of course a very detailed central plan cannot function well in any case, since it is bound to contradict itself in detail. Then as in all tyrannies, much depends on individual personality. To have to work under such wholly irresponsible bosses as Ceausescu or Gierek is bad for any planner's morale. But that, 35 years after Soviet conquest, such people should have been promoted at all, or that theft should be increasing also where there is little inflation, argues a generalised failure of the human element through cynicism and corruption.

Moreover happiness is not a historical constant. There is now in all these countries a fin de siècle feeling: i.e. a cumulation of disappointments. Not just the economy but the whole theocratic system is no good, it perpetuates itself merely by its own inertia. The leaders used to believe in all of it, and the people in about one half. But such favourable circumstances could not last. Much as suppressed inflation has arisen out of the slow cumulation of liquid balances, so suppressed disbelief has arisen out of the slow cumulation of broken promises. The scale of these promises, and their unending crude repetition at the lowest intellectual level, are difficult for a Westerner to imagine. They are of a totally different order of magnitude from the deceptions of Western politicians, and amount to a systematic, overwhelming, diurnal lie.

The result is that the once half-accepted Theocracy has become a 'Logocracy': everyone continues to use the obligatory words in which no one believes, because each is afraid to be the first to use different words and so endanger the whole structure of thought, and his own and his friends' livelihood. The Logocracy still makes enormous moral claims, but they have become totally invalid. In particular it has broken its implied compact with the people: 'shut up,[5] and you'll live securely and a little better every year'. The jobs are still certain but the 'little better' has ceased to arrive. The trade of silence for goulash has become a crude demand for silence alone. The unhappiness that affects economic performance is, therefore, political in origin.

Yet it is extremely dangerous to generalise about these seven countries. Each must be carefully distinguished, and so must the minorities (Georgians, Slovaks, Transylvanian Hungarians) within them. Each has a different history and each is at a different point on what appears to be a common path. Do they, for instance, infect each other? The rulers and their technicians meet constantly, so at that level there must be such infection. The people are quite prosperous enough for tourism, but both security and the shortage of hard currency confine them to each other's countries. There is a very great deal of such tourism, and it is intimately connected with the local black market. So here again there is certainly infection — or, as the rest of them look at 'Solidarity' Poland, revulsion.[6]

Poland is of course no more a Logocracy. Nearly everyone, on all sides, knows and says that the emperor has no clothes, so it is ruled by force alone. The other satellites have arrived, psychologically, where Poland was in August 1980, and it is that 'pre-Solidarity' state that I have been describing. That is the 'Polish Disease' of our title. The subsequent extravagant events will surely not repeat themselves in other countries, if only because everyone can see how terrible in material terms life had become even before 13 December 1981, during the 16 Solidarity months.

A more curious case is the USSR itself. Surely if her revolution came 28 years earlier the Polish Disease must also have set in earlier? Yet it would not appear so. The Great Purge took all the spirit out of people, and then the war united them behind the leadership they happened to have. Listless and downtrodden, they were yet in 1945 a fairly orderly people, afraid to steal or complain, moderately willing to work since their liquid accumulations were small, and fairly sober in view of the vodka shortage. Above all their rulers, unlike say the Czechoslovak rulers, can take pride in imperial, super-power status, and have never lost the 'Orthodox' religiosity traditional in Russian rulers. They are the only self-confident rulers among the seven nations.

So it comes about that all seven are undergoing the same crisis of everyday morale at the same time, with Poland in the lead. But who brings up the rear? Clearly not Romania, USSR or even Czechoslovakia. Can it be the two orthodox, loyal satellites East Germany and Bulgaria?

Growth rates have fallen in both cases, but performance is still respectable, social order more than adequate and planning fairly wise. Contrast for instance the massive movement of Bulgaria into atomic energy with the incredibly unwise choice of Romania to live by converting OPEC crude (see Smith, below). Or consider the bold decision of East Germany to export some of its most violent, loyal and unscrupulous citizens as security policy advisers to Mozambique and South Yemen, despite the continued attractions at home of West German politics, culture and prosperity. Surely they were needed in Leipzig? — the answer seems to be no, dissidence is low, and the risk was well taken.

But is there not another, more surprising, competitor for last place in the Polish stakes: Hungary? A few years ago one would have said,

here is a country hardly less open to Western influence than East
Germany, and which actually went to war with the USSR in 1956.
Yet economic performance is very creditable, except for mild inflation,
and the government is regarded almost with affection. The reasons are
of course the moderate freedom of speech (political cabarets are
exceedingly risqué); the substantial freedom of the arts proper; the
evident determination of the government to be a buffer against, not the
agent of, the USSR; and the extraordinary skill and wisdom of the
economic managers. There is scope for initiative at lower levels (encouraged as we have seen by realism at the top), and at least queues
and suppressed inflation have been avoided; therefore the frustration
felt by, say, Czechoslovak workers and managers has little parallel,
even though both nations are under direct Soviet military occupation
after re-conquest. The quasi-market has lessened alienation and in this
indirect way improved performance. To put it in Drewnowski's terms,
the 'tissue' is on the mend.

No longer! The alienation is still more or less absent, the cabaret
still risqué and, maybe, the economic managers wise. But performance
has fallen off badly and the debt has grown menacingly (see Barker,
here). The inflation is more substantial and there is a vast black economy.[7] Hungary has survived very ill the late oil shock of the CMEA.

I feel, then, partly confirmed in my original quasi-Stalinist insistence
that 'mercatisation' is a Pandora's Box, and must not be treated as an
obviously good thing. It may well contribute to happiness, not necessarily to performance. After all the performance of the USSR during
the NEP was not brilliant, and Britain today is a much more complete
market economy than Hungary. The present Soviet system has shown
tremendous advantages in the past in price stability, tax discipline,
labour mobilisation and sheer development. It is very efficient indeed
at weapons production and weapons research, and in East Germany
and even Czechoslovakia,[8] it has kept advanced economies advancing,
contrary to all expectations. Neither the UK, nor Canada, nor Finland,
nor Sweden can say as much (1977-81).

It is helpful to cast our net still wider. Has Yugoslavia, has China,
caught the Polish Disease? They are not under Soviet command, their
history has been quite different, their institutions differ widely too.
But they have been under Marxist–Leninist monopoly parties since
about the same date as six out of our seven countries. What, too, is the
connection between the British and the Polish Diseases?

Yugoslavia must be pronounced a fellow-victim. Her freedoms, of
both speech and profit-making, are, despite all border-opening and

'mercatisation', felt to be insufficient. Her rate of open inflation has long been the highest in Europe after Iceland's; yet there are still price controls and queues. Her top people are exceedingly corrupt. Her workers use their undoubtedly meaningful powers of self-management for job security, the restriction of hiring and the raising of prices. Her general economic performance has always fluctuated, but these fluctuations are now around a much lower trend. This is, mutatis mutandis, the 'Polish Disease', and most of it has been flourishing for a long time. But Yugoslavia is politically decentralised, and not a member of the Warsaw Pact. So these phenomena can continue without threatening the fall of the central government or a Soviet invasion.[9] Above all Yugoslavia has not for many years been a proper Theocracy; the Party is too pragmatic, the ideology too unassuming and flexible. It is therefore not possible for her to degenerate into a Logocracy. Nor, relying like Hungary on foreign direct investment, is her system so 'unfriendly' to foreign technology. It is not probable that she has reached, or even will ever reach, a 'minimum technology gap'. Her form of the disease, then, is 'desperate but not serious'.

Can such phenomena afflict a very poor Communist country? China is a very large and very localised country, in which almost anything is probably happening somewhere at a moment of time. It should therefore be approached with extreme hesitation. A sort of economic war-lordism is endemic, and instances of not very large peculation now figure in the press. There is also a good deal of sheer civil disorder. But the people as a whole are not self-assertive, and the advantages of new investment and new technology are quite outstandingly obvious – could they but be paid for. Besides, labour morale has substantially improved since the Gang of Four was ousted.

Analogous problems, then, very poor countries have. But it seems misleading to call them 'Polish,' and not all of them suffer at all: we look in vain for them in the 'independent Stalinists', Albania and North Korea.

Should the seven (for even Hungary must be included) reform their economies? For it is evident even to me, the erstwhile protagonist of Stalinist economics, that serious reform must now come, in the direction of the market and decentralisation. This is for human, not economic reasons; for as we have seen the system has tremendous achievements to its credit. But people are simply not willing to work the system any more, and it is too 'discipline-intensive'. Democracy and free criticism simply cannot be allowed, for the detailed plan must be respected. Hence one may wonder whether a slow degeneration of

Drewnowski's 'tissue' was not to be expected in any case, even under a much less Stalinist regime than the Polish.

The disadvantages have almost all been the cumulative consequences of the success of the system. Consider suppressed inflation (Wiles, here): it has crept up year by year because of the system's success in developing small savings. And the alienation: it could not have become so great if the system had not succeeded in spreading education. Then again by simply surviving, yet not completely succeeding at once, the Theocracy has degenerated into a Logocracy. For its creed is false; but the more often it is repeated and tested against reality the more thread-bare it becomes, even if the system that it inspires is not doing badly. Or yet again certain consumer goods are 'counter-revolutionary': wirelesses and television sets for obvious reasons, and motor-cars for the black distribution process (Wiles here). Yet it is the success of the system that produces these antigens in ever greater numbers. It is also that success that produces alcoholic drink and the income to buy it, and generates the tremendous ecological problems for which we seem to have had no space. In respect of these two plagues the USSR is very like any advanced capitalist country − except in its capacity to cope. Finally the need for foreign technology: we see often in what follows the Soviet-type failure to generate new native techniques, but why were the old ones so quickly exhausted? Why is the need for new technology so urgent? − the unemployed have all been put to work.

Let me conclude with the usual Sovietological warning against complacency. Who are we in the advanced capitalist countries to cast the first stone? In particular did not we British contract the Polish Disease long ago? Go back to such a book as 'Suicide of a Nation?' (1963) and read the economic parts,[10] all written by experts from outside the neo-classical tradition. They stress managerial complacency and frivolity (but not corruption); trade union complacency and obstruction; an irrelevant humanist education for top people, especially managers and civil servants; hostility to new technology; the planners' refusal to face reality.

Granted that Marxism−Leninism is a form of humanism, and that British trade unions must reflect their members' opinions, these are exactly the main elements in the Polish Disease. By 1982 we may add inflation − though it is open, not repressed − an inflation that is, as in Poland, unquestionably forced upon, not created by, the monetary authorities, and results from deep popular pressure and indiscipline. There has also been a vast increase in petty corruption, as in Poland; though corruption in high places on a Warsaw scale still seems to be absent.[11]

There are of course plausible and substantial orthodox causes as well: 'stop-go' and the international position of sterling, and now monetarism in high places. I do not seek to decry any of the 'orthodox' explanations, merely to reduce their weight in the total aetiology. Note that such explanations differ strikingly between Eastern European Communism and advanced capitalism, while the 'imponderables' have a striking similarity. But this may be only superficial, since certainly the political causes of low labour and managerial morale are different under advanced capitalism, if indeed they exist at all. For instance the British Disease is commonly dated from the third quarter of the nineteenth century.[12] But a slow international infection, transcending all merely systemic boundaries, is not to be excluded.

Will the Polish Disease go away again, like influenza, or is it here to stay, like rheumatism? Prediction is a hazardous game. Two good Soviet harvests running; a 25 per cent fall in the relative price of oil; the adoption of the Hungarian system by Czechoslovakia (not likely under Husak!); the success of the SALT talks — each of these might make the scene look very different for some countries. But not for all, and for how long? My impression is that these authors, including myself, have not diagnosed the flu.

Notes

1. Workings available on request. I abstract here from the Keynesian economics of a free market, since the Soviet-type economy has no place for Keynes.

2. Thus if the real volume of consumer goods sold grows by 4 per cent p.a., and we save 5 per cent of our incomes, and have nothing to invest our savings in, our liquid stock will outgrow the flow of goods on offer by much more than 1 per cent p.a., because it begins as a much smaller quantity. These very reasonable magnitudes are all derived from Soviet experience.

3. Both the underlying thesis of this section and its qualification are due to Gomulka. See his present contribution.

4. Cf. Amann, 1982, Zaleski et al., 1969. The exceptions are extremely significant: purely intellectual research, as in mathematics and computer software — which do not require physical prototypes and so are independent of the rigid industrial system; and weapons, which benefit from huge financial resources and effective administrative priorities. For the rest the Soviet-type system is 'unfriendly' to R & D.

5. In a Logocracy only the élite, of course, may expound the Logos.

6. The inhabitants of the Soviet empire do not, however, read, view or listen to each other's media very much. Why should they bother?!! Much of their

information in the Western parts of the empire is however derived from the Western media. This includes information on themselves.

7. Though not nearly as big as Hungarian scholars say: see Wiles, 1982. But they may well be right in claiming that the price indices are inflated: see at the head of Ellman here. If so we are bound to conclude that growth has been overstated.

8. The much-touted collapse of the Czechoslovak economy applies only to 1962–4. This was, however, an early example of Communist zero growth.

9. It is a modern commonplace that only countries already Communist, or in the throes of a Communist coup, need really fear Soviet invasion. It is the irreversibility of Communism that the Russians really insist on.

10. Koestler, 1963. The more economic contributors are Goronwy Rees, Austen Albu, John Cole, John Vaizey, Michael Shanks and Andrew Shonfield. Of these only John (now Lord) Vaizey was even grounded in the neo-classical economics.

11. It is of course endemic in local government, where it earns large money by Polish standards (cf. the Poulson case).

12. Shadwell, 1909; Cf. Wiles, 1951.

References

Amann, Ronald in the next 'NATO Annual' (Brussels, late 1982)
Koestler, Arthur (ed.), 'Suicide of a Nation?' (London, 1963)
Shadwell, Arthur, 'Industrial Inefficiency' (London, 1909)
Wiles, Peter in the next 'NATO Annual' (Brussels, late 1982)
Wiles, Peter in 'Oxford Economic Papers' (January 1951)
Zaleski, Eugene et al., 'Science Policy in the USSR' (OECD, 1969)

1 THE POLISH CRISIS: ECONOMIC FACTORS AND CONSTRAINTS*

Domenico Mario Nuti

Introduction

In 1980-1 Poland has been shaken by an unprecedented economic and political crisis. Economic performance, which had already deteriorated in the second half of the 1970s, worsened dramatically. By the end of 1981 Polish national income will have fallen by a quarter in three years, causing a drastic parallel fall in standards of living; persistent external imbalance has led to a mounting foreign debt of the order of $27 billion, which Poland is unable to repay as it falls due; rescheduling of interest and principal repayments is being negotiated with international bankers and Western governments, while Poland has been unable to meet its obligations towards Comecon partners, who have also provided massive aid and finance ($4.2 billion since August 1980 from the Soviet Union alone); there is no prospect of a trade balance being restored before 1986. Open inflation, at 8.5 per cent in 1980 and 15 per cent in the first half of 1981, underestimates internal imbalance in view of endemic and widening shortages of goods, including foodstuffs and basic necessities; one third of current incomes are not matched by goods in the shops and worthless cash piles up in the hands of the population; a wide range of goods are rationed, but rations are not covered and queues lengthen, while patience runs out. About a third of industrial capacity is unutilised because of shortages of energy, materials and intermediate goods; a labour surplus is developing on a vast scale, leading to redundancies, early retirements and emigration, while labour is scarce in some crucial sectors. Central planning and administration is on the verge of collapse. The political crisis is equally acute: social conflict has escalated and is taking the form of strikes, demonstrations, hunger marches; a new 10-million strong Union is in search of identity and acts both like a militant Western-type union and an opposition party; in spite of extensive leadership and government changes, progress towards 'socialist renewal' and democratisation within the Polish United Workers' Party, there is a political stalemate leading to total inaction. Unless the economy starts to recover and social peace is restored soon, the dismal alternatives of either domestic repression

18

or external intervention become increasingly likely.

This essay reviews the basic aspects of the economic crisis, attempts a preliminary analysis of the exogenous and endogenous factors that have caused the crisis, and an assessment of the outlook for economic recovery and the reform of the system. The first part of the essays deals with the second half of the 1970s up to August 1980: the decline in economic performance, its main causes, its political implications, the trigger of the August events. The second part considers developments in the subsequent twelve months, within the Party and the new union, the economic collapse and the economic constraints conditioning recovery and reform. The third part contains some theoretical reflections on the Polish crisis.

Part I: Before August 1980

Deterioration in Economic Performance

In the second half of the 1970s Poland experienced a serious deterioration in economic performance, in spite of the massive accumulation of capital and the large scale import of Western technology and machinery undertaken under Gierek's leadership, especially in the first half of the decade. In particular:

(i) The growth rate of income produced (defined following the standard East European conventions) declined steadily from an average 9 per cent per annum in 1970-5 to 6.8 per cent in 1976, 5 per cent in 1977 and 3 per cent in 1978; early income statistics for 1979 indicated a negative growth rate of -1.9 per cent (IKCHZ, 1980) but have now been revised downwards to -2.3 per cent ('Raport', 1981; negative growth was unprecedented in post-war Poland, indeed throughout Eastern Europe with the exception of Czechoslovakia in 1963). This compares with an average planned growth of 7.3 per cent per annum in the five-year plan 1976–80, subsequently scaled down in the yearly plans. By mid-1980 the modest growth of 1.6 per cent planned for 1980 was unlikely to be fulfilled. The decline in national income distributed (i.e. devoted to domestic consumption and accumulation) is even sharper, as can be easily seen from Table 1.1: while up to 1976 income distributed grew faster than income produced, in subsequent years — primarily due to the burden of repayment of debt incurred in earlier years — income distributed grew more slowly than income produced.

(ii) Part of the decline in performance is due to a fall in agricultural output and adverse natural conditions (particularly in 1975, 1976, and 1980) but an equally significant steady decline can be observed in

Table 1.1: Fundamental Indicators of Economic Development, 1971–80

	1971	1972	1973	1974	1975	1976	1977	1978	1979	1980
	percentage increase with respect to previous years at constant prices									
National income produced	8.1	10.6	10.8	10.4	9.0	6.8	5.0	3.0	-2.3	-5.4
National income distributed	9.8	12.7	14.3	12.1	10.9	7.0	2.7	0.7	-3.4	-5.9
Industrial production sold	8.8	10.2	11.0	11.3	11.0	8.3	6.3	3.6	1.9	-1.2
Gross agricultural output	3.6	8.4	7.3	1.6	-2.1	-1.1	1.4	4.1	-1.5	-10.7
Exports	6.2	15.5	11.6	12.3	8.3	4.4	8.0	5.7	6.8	-4.2
Imports	14.0	21.8	22.8	14.9	4.4	9.6	-0.1	1.5	-0.9	-1.7
Economic effectiveness										
Productivity of fixed capital[a]	1.8	3.8	3.0	1.0	-1.1	-2.6	-4.3	-5.6	-9.6	-11
Labour productivity[b]	6.9	8.6	9.0	8.2	8.3	7.7	5.0	3.3	-1.5	-4
Fixed capital per man	4.9	4.6	5.9	7.1	9.4	10.6	9.7	9.5	8.9	8
Difference between labour productivity growth and growth of capital per man	+2.0	+4.0	+3.1	+1.1	-1.1	-2.9	-4.7	-6.2	-10.4	-12
Structure of % income shares										
Total	100.0	100.0	100.0	100.0	100.0	100.0	100.0	100.0	100.0	100.0
– consumption	72.5	70.4	67.0	64.4	64.8	65.9	68.5	69.2	73.8	79.8
– accumulation	27.5	29.6	33.0	35.6	35.2	34.1	31.5	30.8	26.2	20.2

Notes: a. income produced per unit of fixed capital.
b. in the sphere of material production.
Source: 'Raport' (1981), p. 120.

industrial production, from an average of over 10 per cent in 1971–5 to 8.3 in 1976, 6.3 in 1977, 3.6 in 1978, a modest 1.9 increase in 1979, which picked up in the first half of 1980 but ended with −1.2 per cent by the end of the year.

(iii) These declining growth rates and actual falls in levels of income and industrial production are particularly disappointing in view of the sharp increase in the share of accumulation in national income from an average 25 per cent under Gomulka to peaks of over 35 per cent in 1974 and 1975, and the steady growth of fixed capital per man in subsequent years in spite of the downward trend in the share of accumulation in the second half of the 1970s. The growth of labour productivity has declined since 1976 and actually became negative in 1979–80; the productivity of fixed capital started to grow more slowly from 1973 and steadily fell from 1975 onwards (see Table 1.1).

(iv) Continued trade deficits, especially with Western countries (from a cumulative $303 million in 1961–70 to an average $2.6 billion per year in 1975–8 with the industrialised West) led to mounting hard currency indebtedness. In 1971 net external debt amounted to $1.2 billion, matched by central bank reserves estimated at $1 billion. By 1979 external debt (excluding short term loans) had risen to $20.5 billion, overtaking Soviet indebtedness and taking first place among Comecon countries (see Table 1.2). A more than five-fold increase in imports from the West was matched by a less than four-fold increase in exports, leading to consistently negative balances from 1972 onwards; the burden of debt service (amortisation and interest) grew by 20 times over the decade, absorbing an increasing share of export earnings, from 12.4 per cent in 1971 to 75 per cent in 1979 and 81.8 per cent in 1980. These figures understate the total burden of debt and debt-service by the increasing use of short-term debt, which by 1980 had reached the order of $2 billion, and brought the debt service ratio close to unity (i.e. absorbing total export earnings; according to IMF practice a 40 per cent debt service ratio is regarded as the maximum manageable limit). By 1980, external debt had reached $23 billion, plus $2 billion short term debt, plus an undisclosed amount owed to the Soviet Union and East European countries, estimated (EIU, 1981, n.2) at another $2 billion. This external indebtedness had internal repercussions in the form of growing 'internal exports' (i.e. the sale of imported and exportable goods to the public against foreign currency, including goods in scarce supply in ordinary shops) and a growing government borrowing of foreign currency from Polish citizens, with generous interest payments and provisions for the export of foreign currency to finance

Table 1.2: External Debt and Foreign Trade Proportions

1	1971	1972	1973	1974	1975	1976	1977	1978	1979	1980
	2	3	4	5	6	7	8	9	10	11
Long and medium term debt with advanced capitalist countries at the end of the year, $ bn.	1.2	1.5	2.8	4.8	7.6	11.2	14.3	16.9	20.5	23.0
Increase in debt from year to year, $ bn.	x	0.3	1.3	2.0	2.8	3.6	3.1	2.6	3.8	2.5
Export receipts, from advanced capitalist countries, $ bn.	2.3	2.6	3.4	5.1	5.7	6.1	6.8	7.4	8.4	9.9
Debt service (amortisation and interest $ bn.)	0.4	0.4	0.5	1.0	1.5	2.1	3.1	4.5	6.3	8.1
Percentage ratio between debt service and exports of goods and services	12.4	15.4	14.7	19.6	26.3	34.4	45.6	60.8	75.0	81.8
Import outlays for goods and services from advanced capitalist countries $ bn.	2.0	2.7	4.8	7.2	8.7	8.9	8.6	8.9	10.3	10.3
Trade balance, $ bn.	+ 0.3	-0.1	-1.4	-2.1	-3.0	-2.8	-1.8	-1.5	-1.9	-0.4

Source: 'Raport' (1981), p. 124.

foreign travel; by allowing citizens to borrow Polish zlotys against the security of foreign currency, at a rate of almost four times the official rate and with forfeiture in case of default, the Polish government effectively put a high floor to the black market rate for hard currency and, de facto, engaged in black market transactions with Polish citizens.

(v) Open inflation, an unfamiliar phenomenon since the mid-1950s, appeared; the official cost of living index rose at the following rates (see Rocznik, 1980; the index refers to purchases of consumption goods by the population from the socialised sector):

1971	1972	1973	1974	1975	1976	1977	1978	1979	1980
−1.2	0.0	2.6	6.8	3.0	4.7	4.9	8.7	6.7	8.5

(MRS, 1981)

The price fall in 1971 reflects the reversal by Gierek of the December 1970 food price rises, which triggered the Baltic events and Gomulka's downfall. Similar price rises, reintroduced by Gierek in 1976, were also reversed under the pressure of social protest. Rising inflation rates are due to price rises decreed in less sensitive areas, greater enterprise autonomy in price-fixing since 1974 combined with wage-push and imported inflation, and general pressure on demand. The relative stability of food prices, in spite of rising costs, involved large and rising subsidies from the state budget: from zl. 19 billion in 1971 to zl. 166 billion in 1980.

(vi) Shortages of consumer goods — a familiar feature of central planning, tolerable at times of growing standards of living — became persistent and endemic. Shortages per se indicate simply the presence of excess demand (i.e. a price level lower than in equilibrium) and not necessarily repressed inflation, which is an increase in the degree of excess demand (Portes, 1977). From the data contained in table 1.3 monetary balances of the population appear to have increased by a factor of 4.5 over the decade (corresponding to a yearly growth rate of 16.2 per cent) while sales of goods and services have increased only by a factor of 3 (corresponding to 11.6 per cent a year); cash balances have increased by a factor of 5 (or 17.3 per cent a year). In the absence of any evidence of an increased propensity to save of the population, indeed in the presence of clear signs of a progressive flight from domestic currency (like the rising black market rate for foreign exchange, speculative purchases of durables, or simply non-perishable goods, etc.), we can infer a progressively widening gap between actual and desired monetary balances in the hands of the population; given the stable

Table 1.3: Fundamental Magnitudes Illustrating the Formation of Market Equilibrium (Current Prices, zl. bn)

1	1970	1971	1972	1973	1974	1975	1976	1977	1978	1979	1980	Second half year 1980	First quarter 1981
	2	3	4	5	6	7	8	9	10	11	12	13	14
Sales of goods to the population	395	429	482	544	625	713	813	920	1000	1102	1207	630	309
Sales of services	70	75	82	92	104	119	134	150	162	175	192	98	48
Total goods and services	465	504	564	636	729	832	947	1070	1162	1277	1399	728	357
Dynamics (previous year = 100)	x	108.4	111.9	112.8	114.6	114.1	113.8	113.0	108.6	110.0	109.5	108.0	111.2
Total net incomes	489	543	626	717	824	933	1040	1169	1271	1397	1535	797	447
Dynamics (previous year = 100)	x	111.0	115.3	114.5	114.9	113.2	111.5	112.4	108.7	109.9	109.8	109.6	119.4
Monetary balances of the population													
– Total (zl. bn.)	171	198	239	300	370	435	486	538	600	675	766	766	843
of which – savings	117	137	170	213	264	307	339	376	415	464	500	500	542
– cash	54	61	69	87	106	128	147	162	185	211	266	266	301

Source: 'Raport' (1981), p. 127.

prices of goods in short supply, this indicates repressed inflation. Polish economists distinguish, quite rightly, between inflationary gap ('luka inflacyjna') defined as the difference between yearly intended consumption expenditure and the value of yearly sales, and inflationary overhang ('nawis inflacyjny') defined as the excess liquid assets in the hands of the population, i.e. the cumulated inflationary gaps over the years ('Raport', 1981, p. 8; Sadowski, 1981). Thus as long as the inflationary gap is greater than zero, even if it is falling, the inflationary overhang rises over time. The actual quantification of either inflationary gap or overhang impinges on conjunctures about intended consumption or savings; estimates by the Polish State Planning Commission based on family budgets are said to be higher (at zl. 350 billion in mid-1980) than those by the Ministry of Finance based on the analysis of monetary aggregates (unpublished; apparently by about one third), but there can be no doubt that repressed inflation increased in Poland over the 1970s: shortages extended from food to many other consumption goods of daily use, against a background of unsatisfied demand for durables from housing to furniture or mctorcars. In March 1979 the Ministry of Internal Trade listed 280 products for which demand was difficult to satisfy and the list grew longer in the following year. Apart from popular irritation, shortages have other adverse consequences such as: the ineffectiveness of monetary incentives; the indiscriminate purchase and hoarding of anything handy that consumers might be able to acquire, leading to waste and the inefficient distribution of goods, and causing shortages even of goods available in quantities normally sufficient to satisfy population needs; the rapid growth of black or 'grey' markets in which deficit goods are obtained at a higher price, or through 'connections', position or corruption, most people busily 'fixing' and exchanging each other's purchases. In these conditions the private sector thrived in the old areas of market gardening, handicraft, building and restaurants and in new areas such as motorcar repairs. A 'second' or 'parallel' economy developed, broadly tolerated by the authorities because it actually fulfilled a social need and reduced pressure on 'official' economy. The population resented not only the shortages but the resulting unequal distribution of access to goods and services.

(vii) Inevitably, consumption scarcities spilled over into the supply of materials and semifinished products to enterprises, especially through foreign trade: imports or lower exports of shortage consumption goods competing for foreign exchange with imports of necessary materials and intermediate products. Shortages of production goods, however, were mostly generated by the rapid growth of machinery imports which competed with the importation of current inputs, and. the rising dependence on Western intermediate products which followed from Gierek's policy of technology transfer from the West. Shortages of production goods led to a recentralisation of planning processes, combined with an intensification of informal bargaining processes ('przetargowanie', literally 'auctioning', though by pull and reciprocal favours, not by prices) between enterprises and between central and lower planning authorities; the resulting allocation of shortage goods was not necessarily the most efficient, indeed it led to glaring inefficiencies. Like consumers, firms hoarded excessive amounts of materials in scarce supply (in 1979 for instance, inventories of materials rose by 7 per cent, i.e. almost four times faster than industrial production). Inventories were badly distributed: (in the spring of 1980 the Planning Commission started a survey in 25 sectors in order to establish where in the economy inventories were being hoarded unnecessarily); at the same time, in many sectors inventory levels were not sufficient to sustain continued production levels, shortages being most apparent for paper, rolled steel, copper, plastic materials, cardboard, coal and imported inputs. In the allocation of scarce materials the priority system was extended.

(viii) Recentralisation and central distribution of scarce products, however, did not mean that the 'Centre' had a firm control over resource allocation and macroeconomic processes. The irreconcilable claims of different economic agents and the overambitious conflicting targets set for the economy led to the practical disintegration of central control. There was a proliferation of 'priorities' (exports, essential consumption goods, completion of unfinished investment projects, modernisation, motorisation, housing, armaments) which is a contradiction in terms, priority by definition being attributable to one objective only, and even in that case being difficult to implement in an economy characterised by complex intersectoral links, where the progress of the priority sector could be hindered by the neglect of sectors delivering essential inputs to it. In spite of recentralisation supplies to both enterprises and consumers became increasingly disrupted; the whole economic system, by the end of the 1970s, was subject to tensions and shortages which seriously compromised its efficiency (see Nuti, 1981).

(ix) The shortages, tensions and inefficiencies which visibly afflicted the Polish economy generated mounting pressure for economic reform towards a greater reliance on markets and enterprise autonomy along Hungarian lines. At the same time it created an environment in which economic reform could not be introduced or was bound to fail because the activation of markets does not allow enterprises and consumers to assert their choices and make the economy more efficient – if ever they can – in a situation of persistent disequilibrium. An attempt at economic reform based on the concentration of decisional power at the level of 'large corporations' (Nuti, 1977) was made in 1973–5 but was effectively suspended in the mid-1970s precisely because of growing imbalances which necessitated the reestablishment of central control over investment and wages (Nuti, 1981). Workers' participation in enterprise management, introduced in 1956 and already curtailed by 1958, in the late 1970s became a dead letter following the gradual suspension of elections to Workers' Councils decreed, on dubious legal grounds, by the Central Trade Union Council (CRZZ) in 1975 (see Nuti, 1981) thereby eliminating a formal channel of communication for the expression of workers' views and needs outside Party and Union lines. By early 1980 a new reform project was taking shape, involving not only large enterprises but all 'supply links' (local, sectoral, international), shifting the time horizon of operational planning from the yearly to the five-year plan (by itself an indication of loosening central control), introducing greater initiative for social bodies and agencies and not just enterprises, relying on value indicators and linking wages to productivity growth. The new system was scheduled for introduction in the early 1980s, when tensions and shortages were expected to be overcome, but this expectation was badly disappointed by the mounting economic crisis that progressively disrupted the Polish economy and society, bringing the economic machine to a grinding halt in August 1980.

Exogenous and Endogenous Causes

In the wake of the criticism and condemnation of Gierek's leadership that stemmed from the events of August 1980 the impact of exogenous factors on the Polish crisis has been somewhat underestimated. These factors are both natural and international.

Natural factors were particularly adverse in the second half of the 1970s and in 1980, which a much above average incidence of frost, snow, floods and other natural disasters, which affected food supply, transport, building, and caused further repercussions on the rest of the economy. Some Polish leaders referred to recent years as the seven biblical years of poor harvest. Nevertheless, natural factors can only have had a subsidiary role in a crisis of such proportions. Besides, the impact of natural factors was greatly amplified by policy mistakes, such as the systematic neglect of investment in agriculture and transport, which made these sectors more vulnerable than need be to weather conditions. The poor performance of Polish agriculture, illustrated in Table 1.4 is also due to: (i) the deliberate fall in land cultivated by the private sector, from 75.1 per cent in 1970 to 68.4 per cent in 1980, following systematic purchases by the State Land Fund (PFZ) and reallocations – especially in the mid- and late 1970s – to less efficient state farms, cooperatives and 'agricultural circles' (total arable land also fell by 12 per cent over the decade, following the increasing needs of industrialisation); (ii) the 28 per cent fall in employment in private agriculture, from 4.4 to 3.2 million, especially young men, matched by a modest increase in employment in the socialised sector from 0.8 to 1.1 million, leading to labour scarcity in agriculture; (iii) the non-utilisation of agricultural machinery (17 per cent of tractors and 20 per cent of trailers in 1980) because of lack of spare parts (though the number of tractors rose by a factor of 2.5 to 619,000 over the decade); (iv) the inappropriate price policy held back supply and made the private sector switch from animal to vegetable output and forced the socialised sector to switch to animal production to which it was less suited – a switch which made agriculture more dependent on imported grain and animal feed (see Table 1.5). In transport, the development of railways did not keep pace with the requirements of industrialisation; electrification was slow and public transport in general became increasingly inadequate ('Raport', 1981, section II.A.2 on agriculture and section II.A.5 on transport, Simarupang, 1981).

International factors played a major role in the Polish economic crisis. In theory energy self-sufficiency (indeed surplus, as Poland until 1979 has been a net energy exporter, though net exports have fallen from 24 per cent of domestic use in 1960 to 9 per cent in 1978) and foreign trade planning should have been able to protect Poland from the impact of the international crisis; in practice the specific trade and growth policies followed by Poland, as well as accompanying organisational changes, have laid Poland open to the full blast of the energy crisis, world recession and inflation, and rising interest rates in financial markets.

After Gomulka's basically autarkic policy, Gierek's growth strategy envisaged opening the Polish economy to foreign trade and capital. Borrowing on a large scale from Western countries would enable Poland to modernise its industrial structure, by means of technology transfer, the acquisition of licences and the purchase of advanced machinery, without having to restrain the growth of consumption as Gomulka had done; indeed consumption would also grow out of borrowed funds. The

Table 1.4: Vegetable Output, Use of Fertilizers and Pesticides

	1970	1975	1976	1977	1978	1979	1980
Vegetable output in zl. bn. (at 1976–7 prices)	315.7	346.3	363.4	337.4	355.6	342.3	290.4
Mineral fertilizers (kg. per ha.)	123.6	181.9	193.3	189.0	190.3	188.9	192.9
Productivity of vegetable production per ha. in grain units	25.5	29.4	31.2	29.0	30.8	28.6	24.2
Use of pesticides (kg. per ha.)	0.39	0.58	0.53	0.68	0.51	0.50	0.49

Source: 'Raport' (1981), p. 123.

Table 1.5: Import of Grain and Animal Feed

	1970	1975	1976	1977	1978	1979	1980
Import of grain (000 tons)	2504	3967	6092	5741	7320	7250	7718
of which: from capitalist countries	1348	2829	5701	4650	6740	6575	7278
Import of animal feed (000 tons)	439	1087	1128	1161	1231	1444	1445
Value of total grain and animal feed import in m. currency zlotys' (c.i.f.)	824	2526	3596	3227	3680	4295	5456

Source: 'Raport' (1981), p. 123.

debt thus incurred would be repaid out of higher exports, Polish competitiveness being improved by productivity increases — due both to modernised up-to-date plant and consumption-induced labour incentives. There was talk of 'import-led' and 'consumption-led' growth, and bombastic formulas such as 'Second Poland' (after the First golden-age Poland of Kazimierz the Great), 'intensive and selective development', 'Poles can do anything', now referred to as 'the propaganda of success'. In principle, this kind of policy could have worked, but it was ill-timed, badly executed and overdone.

The timing could not have been worse. The oil crisis started precisely as Gierek's policy went into full swing and, moreover, Poland was engaged in a major industrial reform designed among other things to decentralise enterprise decisions and open the economy to the influence of international prices. The impact of international factors was manifold:

(i) the traditional insulation mechanism from international trade, typical of the centrally planned economy, had been dismantled when it was most needed; international inflation, conveyed to industrial enterprises by means of a new way of measuring enterprise performance at international 'transaction prices' was often imported and built into price formulas, spilling over into wage payments (see Nuti, 1977).

(ii) Prospects for the exports of Polish manufactured goods deteriorated in view of the world trade recession, aggravating external imbalance and leading Poland to step up conventional exports such as coal and foodstuffs.

(iii) the mechanism of petrodollar recycling made it possible for Polish leaders to adopt the easier way out, of raising their indebtedness, instead of adopting unpalatable deflationary measures (Portes, 1981).

(iv) Monetarist policies adopted in advanced capitalist countries to deal with inflation led to a three-fold increase in interest rates; Polish debt being mostly short and medium-term, the increase was immediately reflected in the mounting burden of debt servicing.

(v) Recession in the advanced capitalist countries encouraged Western companies to seek trade with Eastern Europe and to offer attractive terms, but as a result Poland probably was induced to raise imports over what was strictly required by Gierek's import-led growth strategy (an instance is the import of British-made ships, hardly a sector characterised by 'high' technology).

(vi) Although Polish terms·of trade had only registered minor fluctuations around a stationary trend since 1974, due to coal exports, Poland was greatly affected by the disruption caused by the curtailment of oil supplies from Soviet, Iranian and Iraqi sources; also, the oil price rise drastically decreased the competitiveness of the Polish (oil-based) chemical industry.

(vii) The world recession affected adversely the viability of precisely those sectors in which Polish investment had concentrated, such as metallurgy and machine-building.

In view of these factors, Gierek's strategy ran into an extraordinary bout of bad luck. This, however, does not absolve Gierek's team of their responsibility. First, they made a serious error of judgement in grossly underestimating the sheer scale of the world economic upheaval following the energy crisis and, therefore, were caught unprepared (in 1975 former Premier Jaroszewicz declared that the oil crisis was only a minor passing ripple in the development of the world economy and trade). Second, they persisted in their original policy well into the second half of the 1970s in spite of the drastically changed circumstances which totally undermined its plausibility.

The exogenous (natural and international) factors listed above combined and interacted with endogenous ones. The single major domestic cause of the Polish crisis is the scale on which Gierek's overambitious growth policy was pursued, namely the unchecked overaccumulation undertaken in Poland throughout the 1970s. Already under Gomulka capital accumulation was kept at a high regime, rising gently but steadily from 23.1 per cent of national income distributed in 1960 to 25.4 in 1965 and 26.1 per cent in 1970. Under Gierek accumulation was accelerated (see Table 1.1), reaching a peak of 35.6 of national income in 1974, maintained in that neighbourhood in 1975 (35.2 per cent) and 1976 (34.1 per cent), then declining but still over 30 per cent in 1977 and 1978 (31.5 and 30.8 per cent respectively). Accumulation was then drastically cut to 26.2 per cent of national income in 1979, and further to 20.2 per cent in 1980; but the investment cuts in the late 1970s had not been planned beforehand; they were imposed by bottlenecks in construction and installation, and by the reduced import capacity of the Polish economy. As a result, the so-called 'investment front' broadened, i.e. the large number of projects started in the first half of the 1970s were starved of resources for completion, lengthening gestation periods and 'freezing' resources in a form that provided neither means of consumption for the population nor exportable products, frustrating Gierek's policy of modernisation and growth. By 1975 37 per cent of investments completed in the socialised sector had a gestation period above the norm; in 1980, 61 per cent of investments completed had taken longer than planned (84 per cent in building).

The average gestation period in 1980 for completed projects was 35 months, corresponding to a rise by a third with respect of 1975; in industry gestation periods rose by 21 per cent to 47 months from 1976 to 1980. The value of investment resources 'frozen' in unfinished projects amounted to zl. 821 billion (at 1977 prices) by 1980 (see Table 1.6), equivalent to 1.6 times the value of total investment in the same year; frozen resources included zl. 60 billion of machinery and equipment, mostly imported from the West, purchased but not yet installed; almost zl. 1300 billion were already committed to the completion of those projects, rising to 1500 billion if complementary investments (not yet begun but essential to the operation of investment already started) are also considered. The completion of those projects would require from 4 to 5 years, while the comparable period in other socialist countries is 1–2 years.

Capital accumulation in Poland over the 1970s can be said to have been excessive in more than one sense:

(i) with respect to the absorption capacity of the economy, particularly in the building industry, in the construction of plants and the installation of machinery (Kotowicz-Jawor, 1979); as can be seen by the abnormal lengthening of gestation periods that made the projects undertaken much less attractive and wasted — by 'freezing' them — investment resources;

(ii) with respect to the economy's ability to finance the foreign exchange requirements of that accumulation, both for the purchase of machinery and licences and for the provision of recurrent intermediate products and materials necessary for the normal operation of the investment undertaken;

(iii) with respect to the unwillingness of the population to accept the inflationary trends built into the acceleration of investment, as witnessed by popular protests in 1970, 1976 and 1980, which obtained the reversal of price increases and toppled both Gomulka and Gierek;

(iv) with respect to the interests of maintainable consumption, as the increase in income generated by additional investment was mostly committed to the maintenance of the investment drive (Kalecki, 1969);

(v) with respect to the national plan: it appears that in 1971–5 the sum of investment planned by investing agencies ('resorty', i.e. primarily Ministries) exceeded by 15.2 per cent the guidelines of the central plan; in 1976 by 25.8 per cent; investment plans in turn tended to be overfulfilled systematically, with enterprises stepping up their requirements for investment resources once they had succeeded in 'hiking themselves onto the plan' — a tendency which was stronger the·

Table 1.6: Resources Frozen and Committed in Unfinished Projects

	Investment outlays 1971–80 at 1.1.1977 prices		Cumulated outlays on investment projects started but unfinished at 31.12.1980 (frozen resources)		Outlays necessary for the completion of investment projects already started (resources committed)	
	zl. bn.	per cent	zl. bn.	per cent	zl. bn.	per cent
Total socialised economy	4,834.1	100.0	821.2	100.0	1292.7	100.0
Industry	2,176.0	45.0	428.0	52.1	667.4	51.6
of which						
Fuel and energy	502.5	10.4	109.7	13.4	223.9	17.3
Metallurgy	312.3	6.5	65.4	8.0	119.1	9.2
Electro-machine industry	525.4	10.9	92.3	11.2	150.9	11.7
Chemicals	240.5	5.0	69.0	8.4	54.8	4.2
Mining	130.7	2.7	21.2	2.6	35.3	2.7
Wood and paper	96.7	2.0	32.3	3.9	13.4	1.0
Light industry	122.4	2.5	9.7	1.2	19.2	1.5
Food processing "	215.0	4.5	24.9	3.0	46.6	3.6
Building	261.5	5.4	24.8	3.0	25.8	2.0
Agriculture	580.8	12.0	52.3	6.4	56.9	4.4
Forestry	22.1	0.5	1.5	0.1	1.9	1.4
Transport and communications	519.0	10.7	50.0	6.1	91.8	7.3
Trade	121.7	2.5	12.7	1.5	20.7	1.6
Local authorities	230.1	4.8	64.1	7.8	93.4	7.2
Housing and local non-material services	586.9	12.1	116.2	14.2	208.5	16.1
Science and technology	31.7	0.7	4.5	0.5	10.4	0.8
Health and education	86.9	1.8	13.6	1.7	25.9	2.0
Culture and arts	14.3	0.3	3.8	0.5	4.4	0.3
Environment and social assistance	66.9	1.4	18.2	2.2	43.9	3.4
Physical education, tourism and rest	66.2	1.4	14.1	1.7	15.8	1.2

Source: 'Raport' (1981), p. 126.

lower the level at which investment decisions were taken (Kotowicz-Jawor, 1979);

(vi) with respect to the central administration's ability to cope with the tensions and shortages generated by the investment drive, as witnessed by the gradual collapse of central planning and the total disorganisation of the Polish economy in 1980–1.

The second endogenous cause of the Polish economic crisis is the inappropriate and inefficient structure of capital accumulation. Thus if we compare the decades 1961–70 and 1971–80 we find that the share of investment devoted to agriculture fell from 16.5 to 15.7 per cent; investment in social consumption (hospitals, schools, etc.) fell from 28.3 to 23 per cent; while the share of industrial investment rose from 37.8 to 41 per cent. Especially in the years 1976–80 investment was concentrated in the production of investment goods; the structure of unfinished projects is strongly biased in favour of fuels and energy (34 per cent of commitments in industry), electro-machine industry (22 per cent) and metallurgy (18 per cent), with a parallel low incidence of projects oriented towards either exports or the internal consumption market, or technically advanced products (see Table 1.6). Only 20–25 per cent on industrial investment was devoted to modernisation of existing plant (compared with 60–70 per cent in the CDR and in Czechoslovakia), thus neglecting attractive investment opportunities and leading to the dereliction of existing capital. Often the scale of new projects was too large; their location aggravated regional disparities (16 per cent of investment outlays going to the Katowice province, and 8 per cent to Warsaw over the decade) and led to excessive transport-intensity of output. The massive acquisition of foreign licences turned out to be misguided: of 428 licences (mostly in heavy industries) 20 per cent were never used; and 55 per cent only were realised in the planned period; 10 per cent are now said to be unjustified in view of equivalent domestic alternatives; half of the utilised licences turned out to be very import-intensive ('Raport', 1981, pp. 88–97).

Among the many instances of mistaken investment projects, the following projects are now being particularly strongly criticised in Poland:

(i) The Katowice steelworks, started in 1974 outside the five-year plan provisions, uneconomically based on the import of Soviet ores, with a cost overrun of 50 per cent, and 8.8 billion zlotys worth of non-used machinery by 1980; the second stage of the project has been cancelled; (ii) the Massey-Ferguson-Perkins Ursus tractor and diesel engine plant, also started in 1974, expected to start production in 1980 and turn out 75,000 tractors and 15,000 engines a year; in spite of a 100 per cent cost overrun production in 1980 was 2,000 tractors, each tractor requiring $4,000 of imported parts; (iii) the Berliet buses plant at Jelczansk, one of Gierek's pet projects following a licencing and co-operation agreement with France; output in 1980 was expected to be 5,000 but failed to reach 1,000; each bus turned out to have an import content of $6,000, so that Poland had to turn to imports from its earlier partner, Hungarian Ikarus; besides, Berliet buses were unsuitable for the Polish climate and road conditions; (iv) the PVC plant at Wloclawek, a coproduction with the UK company Petrocarbon Development, financed by Lloyds Bank on a buy-back provision; started in 1975, the plant is unfinished (a similar plant in Hungary took four years to construct) and delays have caused chain reactions, such as the non-utilisation of the ethylene produced at Plock by a new plant built by the Japanese which came on stream in time. Similar instances abound. (See 'East-West', 1981; 'Raport', 1981.)

The third endogenous cause of the Polish crisis is incompetence, and negligence, the corruption of individual decision-makers who, in recent months, have been dismissed in large numbers. Thus in May 1980 directors and vice-directors of 84 enterprises in the building industry were dismissed 'for gross neglect of their responsibilities'; 61 directors of state and collective enterprises were also dismissed; many more managers and officials have been dismissed since August 1980. A special Commission headed by Tadeusz Grabski investigated 26,000 charges of misconduct and upheld them in 12,000 cases; it was reported in early July 1981 that 3,500 people had been involved in the illicit construction of private houses and villas; in a Report to the Central Committee Grabski recommended prosecution of Edward Gierek and his Prime Minister Piotr Jaroszewicz.

Political Implications

Economic decline and glaring waste gradually eroded the legitimacy of the Gierek team and the Party itself. It bred disillusionment, cynicism and open dissent. Specific Polish historical and cultural traditions provided a particularly favourable background for organised dissent: a memory of resistance and uprisings against unpopular governments, since the partitions of Poland at the end of the 18th century; class struggles in the inter-war period (in 1923; in the 1930s during the Popular Front movement; a peasant political strike in 1937); resistance during World War II (see Brus, 1980). The Catholic Church provided an alternative set of values and a reference point; it is hard for a Western

European observer to look at the Church as a credible depository of tolerance and pluralism, but this is how it has been seen in Poland since the last War; the role of the Church probably has been over-emphasised — the Polish Church had much to lose and on balance has been a force for conservation and stability — but it has certainly provided a support system, encouragement and inspiration for critics of the regime, especially since Pope John Paul II and his 1979 visit. The Party had been purged of many Stalinists in 1956, when many reforms had taken place (workers' self-management organs, etc.), though these were later withdrawn. A relatively large private sector reduced the power of the state as labour employer; popular upheaval had both brought Gomulka to power in 1956 and brought him down in 1970 (Bromke, 1981).

In the first half of the 1970s Gierek enjoyed popularity due to the circumstances of his coming to power and the steady improvement in living standards. The first signs of open dissent started in the mid-1970s, following Gierek's move to amend the Polish constitution and consecrate the leading role of the Party. On 5 December 1975 the so-called 'Manifesto of the 59' addressed to Parliament by Professor Edward Lipinski and other intellectuals contained political complaints and demands for civil liberties; it was followed by similar protests, allegedly signed, in all, by 40,000 people (Szafar, 1979). Protesters used to sign their names and addresses; the constitutional amendments were passed, but in a much toned down form. In June 1976 a sound but clumsy attempt at price increases, without consultation, led to workers riots in Ursus and Radom, and a general strike. Within 24 hours the price increases had been reversed. Subsequent repression led the signatories of the 'Manifesto of the 59' to set up, on 23 September 1976, a Committee for the Defence of Workers (KOR), linking repre-sentatives of intellectuals and workers. In spite of attacks, KOR main-tained an organised opposition, with continuous petitions, protests, demands for judicial enquiries and compensation, hunger strikes; in July 1977 an amnesty freed the remaining participants of the June riots still in jail and KOR militants (Szafar, 1979). A KOR Information Bulletin appeared, in mimeographed form. In October 1977 KOR re-emerged as a wider Committee for Social Self-Defence (KOR-KSS). Other movements were launched: the Movement for the Defence of Human and Civil Rights (ROPCiO), Student Solidarity Committes, and other minor groupings. In October 1977 fourteen current or past members of the PZPR, headed by former First Secretary Edward Ochab, addressed an open letter to the Central Committee, criticising party policy and calling for political and economic reform; formally this was simply part of pre-congress discussion on the VII Congress theses; some Eurocommunist influence was discernible on a tiny section of the Party. A secret Polish League for Independence (PNN) operated through emigration links. Other groupings were formed, from the so called Democratic Movement to the extreme right-wing group of Leszek Moczulski. A 'Flying University' held alternative lectures in the social sciences. Committees were set up for the Defence of (Catholic) Believers, for the Defence of Peasants, as well as rudimentary and tentative 'Free Unions'. Samizdat publications mushroomed, in spite of paper shortages: the KOR-KSS 'Biuletyn Informacyjny', 'Bratniak', 'Gwzeta Polska', 'Glos', 'Gospodarz', 'Komunikat KSS-KOR', 'Merauriusz Krakowski i Swiatoky', 'Opinia', 'Robotnik', 'Rzeczpospolita'; according to the student paper 'Bratniak' (no. 1, January–February 1979) there were 25 samizdat publications (including a number of single issues) with a circulation of 40,000 a year; 'Robotnik' (Worker), a cyclostiled sheet, was said to have reached a circulation of 25,000 in mid-1980. Semi-official publishing houses were set up, such as NOWA and Zapis, publishing books as well as periodicals; leaflets were countless. This extraordinary intense activity was tolerated by the regime − apart from repeated harassment, confiscations, perquisitions, short arrests − for several reasons: no law was being broken; these activities provided a safety valve; the phenomenon could have been contained, but not wiped out; while the need for Western imports and credits, and the presence of Poles in high places in the West (from Wojtyla to Muskie and Brzezinski) encouraged official tolerance.

The Trigger

The combination of economic crisis and political ferment turned into a deep political crisis in the summer of 1980. For the fourth time (after October 1956, December 1970, June 1976) the crisis was triggered off by an increase in food prices, in particular, meat. It should be noted that price increases were not only a sound economic measure, in view of the widening inflationary gap discussed above, but indeed overdue. Also, the scarcity of meat has been somewhat overstated: meat consumption in Poland increased rapidly from 43 kg per head per year in 1960 to 74 kg in 1980 (see Table 1.7; corresponding British figures of 74 kg in 1960 and 78 kg in 1974/5 are understated and not comparable, because Polish data include fat, bones and offal, but the Polish trend is impressive). The main problems with meat supply have consistently been the excessively low price, inefficient distribution over time

Figure 1.7: Basic Indicators of Production and Allocation of Meat and Fats

		1979	1980	1980
		000 tons		(1979 = 100)
1.	Butchered cattle	3,264.5	3,148.1	96.4
2.	Export of live animals, meat, meat products and fats	278.3	248.7	93.6
2.1	of which to capitalist countries	258.9	244.8	94.6
3.	Imports of meat, meat products and fats	9.1	60.3	662.6
4.	Consumption of meat, meat products and fats of which	2,866.2	2,912.8	101.6
	4.1 Meat, processed meat and offals	2,574.4	2,633.6	102.3
	of which: from state supplies	2,171.5	2,220.7	102.3
	from private sources	402.9	412.9	102.5
	4.2 Fats	291.8	288.2	98.8
5.	Consumption of meat, poultry and offals per head (per kg)	73.0	74.0	101.4
	of which – from state supplies[a]	61.6	62.4	101.3
	– from private sources	11.4	11.6	101.7

Note: a. State retail trade, restaurants, nurseries, hospitals, etc.
Source: 'Raport', (1981), p. 128.

and across regions, poor refrigeration facilities, low quality, high consumption by peasants. The price increase was decreed on 1 July 1980, in a more subtle form than on previous occasions: since 1977 a dual price system for meat had been established, whereby 'commercial' state shops sold meat without queues and in sufficient quantities at prices considerably higher than the heavily subsidised normal state shops where meat was in short supply. 'Commercial' sales reached 8 per cent of total sales in 1978 and 18 per cent in 1979; on 1 July the sale of better quality meat was transferred to 'commercial' shops, thereby raising the average price of purchases by the public. The price of sugar, which had been rationed since May, and other foodstuffs, was raised. A wave of strikes followed, leading to compensatory wage increases and further strikes. The new elements of the August strikes, with respect to earlier workers' protests, were the occupation of factories, the link with intellectuals in an advisory role, and the articulation of a long list of specific demands. On 31 August 1980 after long negotiations a settlement was reached at Gdansk, with major economic and political concessions: wage increases, the legalisation of strikes, a new self-managed independent Union, and greater civil and political rights. Gierek was deposed in the same way as Gomulka, and Polish economic and political life took a sharp turn.

Part II: After August 1980

The New Union

Since August the new 'Solidarity' union has been officially recognised and registered, after a legal battle; it has enrolled about 10 million members, including one million (i.e. one third of) Party members; it was joined in May 1981 by a 2.5 million strong 'Rural Solidarity' representing private peasants (demands by Polish policemen to form their own Solidarity branch, however, were promptly quashed by the government with the dismissal of union militants). It has stepped up its demands, through legal proceedings and negotiations, backed by work-to-rule, strike threats, strikes, hunger strikes, demonstrations, marches and a barrage of new publications. A new good quality weekly was launched; in early May Solidarity was granted access to television and radio time for running its own programmes in socio-economic issues and announcing its resolutions and declarations. Its organisational structure is unusual, in that it is regionally based instead of being organised by trade and by sector; this makes it independent from its central committees, which is a source both of strength and centrifugal forces (see Pelczynski, 1981). Since May an information and consultation 'Siec' (Network) has been established between the union branches of 17 large plants, which in early July took the initiative of producing draft legislation on workers' self-management, renaming state enterprises as 'social enterprises' and demanding workers' rights not to participate in management but to manage themselves, to appoint enterprise directors and limit their power to a purely executive role, and obtain a share in enterprise income ('Siec', 1981). By the end of July, over 1,000 self-management organs of various description were spontaneously set up. (In July employees of the Polish Airlines LOT proposed the appointment of their nominee as the new director, striking over the issue, until a compromise solution on top management was found.) De facto, this gave the Union the power of veto both at the enterprise level over management decisions and at the national level over majority policy issues (such as wages, prices, economic reform, etc.).

The new Union's identity is not yet defined. Since last August Solidarity has been playing, in different proportions, three conflicting roles:

(i) that of a political opposition party, without a realistic prospect of taking over from the existing government but effective in putting forward and obtaining political concessions, such as some of those won in the Gdansk agreement of 31 August 1980: press freedom and access to media, restoration of rights of political victims, end of police privileges, end of political nominations to managerial appointments, etc.;

(ii) that of a militant Western-type Union, putting forward impossible economic demands, such as full pay to strikers, lower retirement age for women to 50 and for men to 55; 3-year maternity leave; or the combination of stabilisation of market supply and massive wage increases (28 per cent in the twelve months since August 1980), pension increases and wage indexation; or demands which though perhaps overdue are not compatible today with economic recovery, such as increases in social consumption, better housing, free Saturday and a shorter working week — all concessions also won with the Gdansk settlement;

(iii) that of a genuine socialist-type union, and potential partner in government, as witnessed by demands for an end to foreign currency and 'commercial' sales, the endorsement of rationing, the bid to influence government accumulation policy, or to control food distribution.

There have been undoubtedly syndicalistic tendencies within the new union, as witnessed by the miners' claim that they should decide the allocation of coal and trade it off for food in transactions with the agricultural sector (Staniszkis, 1981), or by Siec's flirtations with group ownership (see Siec, 1981, and below, the section on workers' self-management).

The contradiction between these roles, already present in the demands successfully negotiated in the Gdansk agreement ('Protokoly', 1980), has continued to date, with alterations in its dominant role: for instance, economic militancy at the end of March 1981 was followed in early May by calls for higher food prices, and by self-imposed curbs in Solidarity's radical publications towards the end of June, followed by a revival of economic militancy and opposition to price rises and ration cuts at the end of July. These alternative roles also correspond to deep divisions within the Union, where — amongst other divisions — Lech Walesa's 'centrist' wing has to deal with a more 'radical' wing. Their advisors are equally divided.

On balance, the new Union seems to have taken the road of economic militancy, close to the operation of a Western type union. This is clearly the best course for the survival and strengthening of the new fragile Union structure, as a short term posture in the face of a government reluctant to make concessions. Moderation, or even consistency, are not necessarily virtues in politics; in a diametrically opposite situation, the Italian Communist Party confronting the Catholic monopoly of power has lost, since 1976, both face and people's support by acting in a responsible and accommodating fashion at a time of national difficulties; the lesson is not lost on Solidarity's leaders, who see the risk of 'institutionalisation', or absorption into the establishment, if they choose the role of a potential partner in government. However, there are two important systemic differences which condition the activity of unions in a capitalist and a socialist system:

(i) wage and price demands incompatible with the maintenance of accumulation, or even demands for real wages higher than labour product, in a capitalist system are a bid for the transfer of capitalists' wealth to the workers; in a socialist system this would imply either sales of shares to the public or disposal abroad of national assets. Therefore, militant demands involve the transfer of ownership from the state to individuals or groups, which – if asserted with conviction and persistence, instead of being a temporary posture – is a direct challenge to the socialist system, in that the realisation of these demands would imply private or group ownership of part of the means of production; thus, whatever the intentions of the new Union, it would be disingenuous to deny that economic militancy is not effectively an 'anti-socialist' move;

(ii) the strength of the new Union is, ultimately, the full employment policy to which the socialist government is committed, unlike its counterpart in the capitalist system; full employment (and strikers on full pay) are incompatible, in the long run, with strong economic militancy, and either full employment or militancy will have to give way.

The Party: 'Socialist Renewal'

A major effect of Solidarity's emergence and growth has been the adoption of a policy of socialist 'renewal' ('odnowa') by the Polish United Workers' Party, i.e. effective moves towards extensive democratisation of Party life. It is not a case of 'infiltration', but of competition in the provision of the democratic processes needed by the population.

In preparation for the extraordinary IX Party Congress (which normally would not have been due for another four years), Consultative Commissions (KK-POP) were set up locally, uniting party organisations and establishing 'horizontal links' by-passing central organs. Under pressure from below, within the Party, proposals for the accountability of full-time officials and elected representatives, for multiple choice in party elections and the secret ballot emerged and were gradually established, giving substance to the move towards renewal (See Kolan-kiewicz, 1981). This policy was officially endorsed by Gierek's succes-sor, First Secretary Kania, in spite of open Soviet disapproval (see Brezhnev's letter of 5 June 1981) and strong opposition by Party hardliners (as witnessed by the formation of groupings such as the Katowice Forum and the Grunwald Group, and the attempt to oust Kania at the emergency Plenum of the Central Committee on 9–10 June).

At the IX Extraordinary Congress of 14–19 July most of the promi-nent leaders were elected as delegates, following Kania's call on party activists to return the present leadership intact so that it could be judged by the Congress, and the successful allocation of 'safe seats' to less popular leaders, but the new democratic processes resulted in un-precedented personnel change. Over 90 per cent of the 2,000 delegates were taking part in a party congress for the first time (only 20 per cent of the delegates were blue collar workers; 20 per cent were estimated to be Solidarity members, only 5 per cent were women). Only 23 per cent of former Central Committee members were reelected as delegates. The Congress condemned past policies and leaders, settled accounts, stripped Gierek and others of their honours and endorsed prosecutions of corrupt officials; delegates voiced sharp complaints and put forward bold proposals. The new enlarged 200-strong Central Committee, elected after frank and close questioning of candidates, contained only eighteen former members, excluding even many former Politbureau members and many provincial secretaries. Out of the fifteen members of the new Politbureau only four were reelected, including Kania and Premier Jaruzelski. The Party has ridden the storm, and comes out of the experience considerably strengthened and with greater authority.

Economic Collapse

Since August 1980 the Polish economy has deteriorated much further, turning crisis into collapse. Industrial output, which had been growing by 5.1 per cent in the first half-year, fell substantially in the second half-year, recording an overall decline of 1.2 over the year; gross agri-cultural output also had a very bad year, with a 10.7 per cent fall with respect to the already poor 1979 level; national income produced fell by 5.4 per cent (against earlier estimates of a fall of 4 per cent, and a target increase of 1.6 per cent in the yearly plan). Table 1.8 gives a month by month account of economic decline from July 1980 to April 1981, with a significant drop in August, due to the strikes, a small recovery in September followed by a steady decline, especially in coal,

Table 1.8: Basic Indicators of Economic Development, July 1980–April 1981

	First half year[a]	1980 VII	VIII	IX	X	XI	XII	I	1981 II	III	IV
		corresponding month in the previous year = 100									
Production sold in socialised industry	105.1	100.3	88.2	95.2	92.8	91.5	91.6	90.3	90.3	90.4	87.5
of which:											
coal	102.6	105.1	102.6	79.7	84.7	79.8	86.4	77.8	78.5	81.2	82.0
sulphur	109.9	108.0	109.7	100.8	113.5	109.9	89.7	106.2	88.9	86.3	94.1
copper	115.0	103.8	100.8	111.6	96.1	86.8	89.5	99.8	90.6	87.8	91.8
fertilizers	97.5	90.4	102.5	106.0	87.2	83.6	74.4	106.6	102.7	114.2	93.7
cement	111.5	86.0	82.2	92.1	80.7	92.4	52.6	52.9	72.0	81.4	92.4
Meat procurement	97.9	91.0	84.2	88.8	95.8	92.9	104.5	93.2	88.6	75.8	85.0
Milk procurement	108.7	98.9	95.8	96.1	93.6	88.4	82.0	81.6	77.0	81.3	81.7
Exports	115.0	114.9	88.5	96.9	88.6	90.0	87.6	77.6	79.5	78.7	93.3
of which to socialist countries	102.2	104.4	89.6	92.4	85.6	85.4	84.4	76.6	87.1	82.3	100.3
to advanced capitalist countries	133.6	127.6	87.1	102.4	92.9	95.5	91.8	78.8	71.8	74.7	85.6
Imports	117.7	115.8	99.2	100.6	106.1	96.0	91.2	99.6	101.4	97.9	93.6
of which from socialist countries	111.2	106.2	120.8	120.2	119.1	105.8	103.6	103.8	127.9	116.5	104.6
from advanced capitalist countries	125.1	130.1	79.9	81.9	92.9	85.6	81.1	87.0	79.8	83.2	81.7
Labour productivity in industry	105.2	100.2	88.6	95.9	93.5	92.0	92.2	90.8	90.7	90.7	87.6
Average industrial wage	112.6	110.1	108.9	116.4	120.4	117.6	124.4	117.9	120.0	127.7	127.4
Population incomes allocated to the purchase of goods and services	112.5	108.7	100.7	109.8	107.7	106.8	109.3	110.1	113.3	110.6	115.1
Market supply of goods at current prices	111.4	104.9	95.8	103.4	101.9	100.8	96.9	101.2	101.9	99.1	103.2

Notes: a. To some extent the index for the first half of 1980 is affected by the low basis for the first half of 1979, when the economy suffered production losses due to an exceptionally hard winter.
Source: 'Raport' (1981), p. 121.

foodstuffs, and exports to Western countries, while labour productivity declined and the average industrial wage rose sharply: respective rates of change between April 1980 and April 1981 are −12.4 for productivity and 27.4 for average industrial wage, widening the inflationary gap. Coal output, crucial for electricity generation, industrial fuel and export earnings, dropped only 3.9 per cent over the year, but both exports and stocks were down by more than a quarter over the year (Table 1.9).

Half-year statistics released at the end of July indicate a further sharp fall in economic indicators. Money wages rose by 26 per cent outstripping the official cost of living which increased by 15 per cent. Food prices rose by 14.3 per cent and consumer durables by 8 per cent. The resulting increase in real purchasing power, however, was not matched by actual consumption, as consumer goods supply dropped by 10 per cent over the same period. Meat supplies declined by 17 per cent. The inflationary gap led to a 17 per cent increase in savings, almost all of which is regarded as 'forced' savings in view of the population's already excessive holdings of cash balances not matched by consumer goods in the market. A generalised 'flight from money' has led to a search for durable goods and other inflation hedges, not only jewels but any form of non-perishable and storable goods. The black market rate for hard currency has soared, and has now reached 250 zlotys per dollar, compared to the official rate of 33 zlotys and to a black market rate of 120 twelve months ago. Shortages however have spilled over into the special foreign currency shops 'Pewex' ('Enterprises for internal exports') where hard currency can be spent freely for a limited range of scarce commodities (including food, alcohol, cigarettes, cosmetics, etc.). Industrial production has fallen by 12.5 per cent in the first half year; coal output has fallen 22 per cent to 88 m. tons, and copper output by 11 per cent; oil refineries output dropped 19 per cent leading to several petrol shortages. Despite the sharp fall in industrial output, employment fell by only 0.3 per cent, while electricity consumption was only 1.6 per cent lower. Animal feed supplies dropped by 14 per cent, resulting in a 7 per cent decline in the cattle and a 13 per cent drop in the pig population, involving bleak prospects for future meat supplies. Exports to the West fell by 21.5 per cent and imports by 21.8 per cent, giving rise to a foreign exchange deficit of $150 million (EIU, 1981, no. 3).

Short-term prospects are bleak beyond belief. A government Report on the state of the economy ('Raport', 1981), presented to Parliament and to the Party Congress in mid-July, envisages a dramatic and

Table 1.9: Coal Output, Export and Deliveries (in million tons)

	1979	1980	1980 1979 = 100
Resources			
1. Total from domestic sources	202.6	194.7	96.1
from which			
− coal	201.0	193.1	96.1
− production of briquettes	1.6	1.6	97.6
2. Other sources (stocks, coke imports etc.)	1.0	3.4	340.0
Total resources	203.6	198.1	97.3
Uses			
1. Total domestic supply of which	160.9	167.1	103.9
− for industrial users	127.0	130.5	102.8
of which			
− for electricity general	44.0	47.2	107.3
− production of coke	25.4	25.3	99.6
− other industries	57.6	58.0	100.7
2. Ministry of Communications	3.8	3.7	97.4
3. Other users	0.9	1.0	111.1
4. Supply to the population of which	29.2	31.9	109.2
− CZSR 'Peasant Self-help'	22.8	24.9	109.2
5. Export of which	41.4	31.0	74.9
− to socialist countries	14.7	10.9	73.7
− to advanced capitalist countries	26.7	20.1	75.6
Total uses	203.6	198.1	97.3
6. Total stocks at the end of the year	9.6	7.1	74.0

Source: 'Raport' (1981), p. 122.

unprecedented fall of national income produced by 15 per cent (though later estimates indicate a fall of 17 per cent); industry, officially estimated to operate at 25 per cent below capacity, is expected to reach one third unutilised capacity by the end of the year. Expected bumper harvests might be partly wasted because of shortages of harvesting machinery and processing plant. Meat rations, which in mid-July had been reconfirmed until September, by the end of the month had been cut by 20 per cent from the former average level of 6 pounds per head per month. The cut intensified social unrest, leading to further strikes, hunger marches and demonstrations, and demands for the reinstatement of earlier ration levels (EIU, 1981, no. 3). Official statements in July, from the Chairman of the Price Commission to the First Secretary, have already intimated that massive price increases for consumption goods are unavoidable, with foodstuffs going up by over 100 per cent and some goods like bread and milk going up by 200–300 per cent (with partial wage compensation especially for the lower paid), and that the later prices are raised the higher the rise will have to be. The government however is unable to introduce the overdue price rises without prior negotiations and consent on the part of the Solidarity Union. Since last March Poland has suspended the repayment of its $27 billion as it fell due, paying only interest, and avoided default only because of Western bankers' reluctance to call in their loans and acknowledge their losses. Following the signing of a $2.6 billion debt rescheduling for 1981 between Poland and its 15 Western Government creditors at the end of April (involving a four year grace period) negotiations are pending on the rescheduling of $3.1 billion debt with Western bankers, maturing this year; talks for the rescheduling of debt falling due in 1982 and 1983 will start soon. Meanwhile, Poland has been almost totally starved of short-term credit, while $2.5-3 billion fresh credits are needed to maintain the 1980 level of industrial output. Soviet aid and finance to Poland in eleven months since August 1980 is estimated by Minister Jagielski at $4.2 billion; further aid and finance has been provided by other East European countries, while Poland has not honoured its commitments to Comecon and has negotiated a reduction in its deliveries for 1982-5.

In mid-July a document entitled 'Government Programme for overcoming the crisis and stabilising the national economy' ('Program', 1981) produced by the State Planning Commission, was presented to Parliament and discussed at the IX Congress. The programme envisages seven major areas for government action: raising agricultural output, rationalising the use of raw materials and intermediate goods, increasing domestic production of materials and fuels, maintaining essential imports, stimulating the use of by-products and local resources, activating small scale production and improving and rationalising transport. There are no macroeconomic targets, however, and the programme is short on policy measures, apart from price increases, budgetary cuts, suspension of investment projects, renegotiation of debt and trade commitments, redeployment of labour, and economic reform. The realisation of this vague programme is left to the yearly plans of 1981-5. The programme envisages consultations with the unions to seek a consensus on labour, wages and prices. Without Union endorsement, the programme does not have any chance of implementation. Efficiency measures and economic reform, in fact, would involve – together with the investment cuts and difficulties with imported supplies – massive redundancies of the order of 1.2 million, which would have to be negotiated (schemes for early retirement, redundancies on part-pay and labour redeployment from heavy industry to mining and agriculture have already been announced; emigration is also on the increase).

The sheer scale of economic collapse can only in a small part be imputed to labour militancy and the August settlement. The combination of wage increases and lower supplies is responsible for the widening inflationary gap, queues and rationing, and disruption in the consumption market; the miner's free Saturday has cost precious export earning, with multiplier effects on the rest of the economy. But the main causes of the 1981 collapse are the combination of Poland's extraordinary import-dependence on the West — from distilled water for car batteries to steel cans for food processing — and the loss of short-term credit facilities (of the order of $2 billion) on which Poland had been relying for essential imports, following the suspension last March of debt repayment and pending negotiations for debt rescheduling. Other contributory factors have been the continued disintegration of central planning and administration, the paralysis of decision-making at all levels; the political stalemate that blocks even obvious emergency measures.

The Road to Recovery

If Poland were a capitalist country in a similar crisis, painful but fairly automatic processes and policy response would be set in motion. There would be hyperinflation, currency devaluation, drastic public expenditure cuts and deflationary taxation measures, tight money, high interest rates, disinvestment, bankruptcies and plant closures, and a couple of million unemployed. Some external creditors would get very little, or nothing at all, following the financial collapse of their debtors; some of the remaining debt would be offset by the sale to foreigners of financial assets (shares, bonds), land, buildings and plant. Fresh external finance would be available to the more credible borrowers. Unemployment would keep the unions in check, restraining real wages and ensuring labour discipline. The drop in real wage trends and industrial streamlining would eventually promote exports and encourage new investment, attracting foreign capital; in ten years or so the economy would be getting out of the crisis.

Polish systemic features may avoid some of the more unpleasant aspects of this scenario, but they add constraints which make recovery much harder: there are no liquid assets to market abroad; the government being the ultimate borrower, lenders have difficulties in discriminating between the viable and non-viable sections of the Polish economy; there is no bankruptcy, in the conventional sense, for a sovereign government, thus no relief through the cancellation of debt;

an even modest commitment to social welfare and job security adds to total claims on existing resources; moreover, recovery mechanisms based on self-correcting changes in interest or foreign exchange rates are not automatic. All this calls for an even heavier reliance on the policy measures demanded by economic recovery: austerity, in line with the recent economic decline and to make room for the repayment of debt; large price rises and possibly continued inflation, to normalise consumption markets and eliminate time-consuming queues (realistic rations, in the shorter run); harder and longer labour, to compensate for scarce materials and productivity falls; economic reorganisation, to avoid inefficiency in the use of resources.

There is no sign that the first three necessary policy measures (austerity, inflation, greater intensity and length of labour) are acceptable to the Polish people. Austerity and inflation are deeply resisted. The more radical wing of the Solidarity Union demands 100 per cent indexation of the present wage level, as a precondition for accepting price rises. In view of the inflationary gap for compensatory wage rises to be matched by goods in the shops the consumption level would have to increase by 20-5 per cent, which is out of the question. Even then, the present excess of purchasing power in the hands of the population (which would be reduced but not eliminated by the envisaged price rises) would have to be either taxed away or consolidated in long term government bonds, for equilibrium to be restored in consumption markets. A convenient way of restoring equilibrium in consumption markets would be a currency reform like that executed in Poland and in other East European countries in the 1950s, converting money wages, prices, savings and cash at differential and unfavourable rates into new units, reducing both the real value of liquid wealth (at a progressive rate) and real wages it seems unrealistic, however, to expect the present government to obtain consensus on this highly unpopular measure. Without the taxation or consolidation of excess cash, even the substantial price rises currently under negotiation will not eliminate queues and shortages for perhaps another five years. The reduction of rations is a necessary step for rationalising distribution, but has led to fierce resistance.

The majority of the population do not seem to understand the connection between the country's economic situation and their own individual consumption. Their past experience of 1956, 1970, 1976 and 1980 leads them to believe that in similar circumstances protest can succeed in keeping prices down, reversing price rises and even raising their consumption (as happened in the early 1970s). They believe that their standard of living can be raised by government decree and impute imbalance and shortages to deliberate choice by a government that could decide otherwise. They are right in blaming *past* government policies but will have to come to terms with current economic constraints, which leave no choice to their government. Others are less naive, but keep up economic pressure as a political weapon, to keep the government on the straight and narrow path to 'renewal', to consolidate achievements, or simply to oppose the present system. Generalised discontent affects labour discipline, in the general sense of unwillingness to work harder and longer, as witnessed by strikes, overtime bans, claims for shorter working time and better working conditions. In these circumstances the entire burden of getting out of the crisis is made to rest solely on the economic reorganisation of the planning system and the functioning of enterprises, i.e. on 'economic reform', which alone is quite inadequate to this task.

Economic Reform and Workers' Self-management

Since August 1980 seven competing projects for economic reform have been produced in Poland: by the Polish Economic Association (PTE, 1980), by a Government-Party Commission for Economic Reform set up in September 1980 (KPZdsRG, 1981a, 1981b), Warsaw University (Moskwa, 1981), the Warsaw Central School of Planning and Statistics (Balcerowicz, 1980), the Wroclaw Economic Academy (AEW, 1981), the Central Technical Organisation (NOT, 1981) and — implicit in fragmentary form and draft legislation — Solidarity circles (Jozefiak, 1981; Siec, 1981; for a preliminary comparative analysis, see Kramer 1981). All projects envisage, to various degrees, the strengthening of social control over the economy; 'marketisation' ('urynkowiente'), i.e. greater decentralisation of economic decisions to enterprises, backed by a revamped banking system, bidding for resources and selling their products instead of executing central directions; and forms of workers' self-management.

The most authoritative set of proposals is that of the Party-Government Commission; assisted by a 500-strong body of experts and political representatives, it produced in July the second draft of a reform project, accompanied by draft legislation on state enterprises and on workers' self-management (KPZdsRG, 1981b). The project is still a consultative document, but gradual implementation is expected to be swift: in the third quarter of 1981, further discussions and finalisation of details, and preliminary laws and decrees; by the end of the year, enterprise reorganisation and establishment of workers'

self-management organs; a reform of supply prices by 1.1.1982, pre-
ceded by the reform (increase) of retail prices, with part-compensation;
from 1982, gradual dismantling of central controls and transition to the
new system in three years, under the supervision of a new Plenipoten-
tiary Minister for Economic Reform (KPZdsRG, 1981b, pp. 52–60).

In the official project the socialisation of the planning process rests
on changes in enterprise regime (self-financing, self-management, independence) and on the clearer definition and reduction of Party
influence on economic life. The Party is said to fulfil (i) the strategic
function of acquainting itself with the most important social interests
and elaborating them in the form of long term party programmes,
'persuading society of their strategic validity' − a function exercised
by the Party Congress and Central Committee; (ii) an 'inspirational'
function, 'at all levels of decision-making thanks to the activity of
party members'; (iii) a controlling function, checking on the implementation of strategic tasks and fighting technocratic and bureaucratic
deviations as well as sectoral and regional particularism (ibid., p. 11).
The Party should not interfere with current operational management,
with technical choices, and with the appointment of managers and
officials (ibid., pp. 11–12).

The central plan is no longer to contain direct commands, except in
centralised investment (budget-financed social infrastructure and large-
scale projects in key sectors), defence and the fulfilment of international agreements. 'The economy will operate on the principle of
central planning with the utilisation of the market mechanism' (p. 21).
Branch Ministries in industry are to be merged into no more than two
or three, possibly one as the Hungarian system (a first step in this direction was taken in early July, with the merging of eleven industrial
Ministries into five). Enterprises are to be independent and self-financing and able to use own and borrowed resources at their discretion;
their investment is no longer planned from the centre, only forecast
in the national plan. Enterprises decide on pay policy, the scale and
assortment of output, supply links and sales policy, investment,
modernisation, research; they can freely associate, merge, set up new
enterprises and − a most important innovation − diversify their activity
into any sector of the economy. Enterprises are expected to 'satisfy
social needs at minimum cost' by aiming at 'profit maximisation'
(p. 32).

There is some naivete in these provisions (and even more in some of
the other projects): vetting of enterprises' plans by banks for the
provision of credit will simply transfer to the banking system the

functions formerly undertaken by central planning organs; probably the same people will continue to exercise these functions, after being re-deployed from planning to banks. The almost Friedmanite confidence on the virtues of markets, prices and profits will amaze Western econo-mists from Keynesians leftwards, advocates of direct controls and intervention; the standard methods of wartime economy might seem better suited to the emergency state of the Polish economy. However, the official project contains specific provisions for the maintenance of central allocation for shortage goods during the transition period, as well as the extensive use of indirect instruments of fiscal and monetary policy for steering enterprises in the general direction of the national plan, while the role of Parliament in the formulation and execution of plans is considerably increased. Moreover, the direct controls and central allocation of wartime economics can be effective when they are introduced in a normally functioning market economy to mobilise resources for a specific task, but their effectiveness is questionable in a crisis economy which is totally disorganised precisely because of the disintegration of central administration and control. There is a great deal of scope for the overhauling of markets and prices in Poland, and for reforming a system whereby steel is produced which is worth less than the energy used up in its production, bread is sold at a price which is a third of the cheapest animal food and widely used as such, and the lack of one dollar for essential imports leads to a loss of output at least ten times greater. There is no reason why a price reform should be delayed until the realisation of enterprise reform and the restoration of equilibrium. A greater reliance on enterprise independence and markets is perhaps a justifiable act of faith, a shock therapy, where everything else has failed. So far only a 'mini-reform' has taken place ('Uchwala', no. 118/80; Nuti, 1981), followed in early July by the liberalisation of small scale production and state farms. Further 'marketisation' will require close and careful monitoring, but is unavoidable.

Economic reform has a double link with workers' self-management, because enterprise independence creates the scope for workers' deci-sional power, and workers' control is the political price that the govern-ment is asked to pay for agreement on the price reform necessary to that independence. The official project firmly reasserts state ownership, one-man management and central appointments, limiting workers' self-management to a conventional role; Solidarity's Siec (Network) goes much further (see above, the section on the new Union). Negotia-tions are open on this crucial issue, while the 1956–8 legislation on workers' councils, now a dead letter, remains formally in force and spontaneous self-management committees are formed.

Current Prospects

The only solution to the political and economic crisis is for the government and unions to reach a Social Pact, similar to the Gdansk agreement of August 1980 but — unlike it — feasible within the very tight constraints of Polish debt and decline. This renegotiated settlement would have to contain provision for austerity, price rises and a long truce in industrial relations, paving the way for stabilisation and reform; in exchange, the new Union could obtain a tangible form of workers' self-management, and the consolidation of those political and civil rights already achieved. Western governments and banks could assist by providing economic aid and fresh loans, on condition that such compromise and new settlement is reached, instead of concentrating obtusely on demands for economic reform *per se* and for stabilisation plans. Without union endorsement of unpopular measures no stabilisation plan is worth the paper on which it is written. The Social Pact might be more credible if a new government of national unity were formed, with Union experts in ministerial posts — though this might not be supported by either the Union's radical wing nor the Soviet Union.

The alternative is an authoritarian solution. Soviet armed intervention cannot be ruled out; Soviet acquiescence is bound to have limits; although previous expected thresholds of Soviet tolerance have been overstepped, this does not mean that there are no limits, or that there could not be a delayed reaction. However, the prospect of Soviet intervention has been overstated: the costs would be very high, due to Polish debt, Soviet and East European own needs for Western finance and dependence on Western technology and grain, existing commitments in Afghanistan, the reluctance of East-European allies, adverse repercussions in the West and Third World; benefits are scant, in view of likely Polish resistance and the sheer scale of the Polish crisis. Besides, the Soviet strategic position is not under serious threat, Poland is still communist and a member of the Warsaw Pact and there are still powerful economic levers in Soviet hands in view of Polish dependence on Soviet supplies, including almost 100 per cent of Polish imports of oil. An authoritarian solution will take the form of internal repression, a clampdown on organised political opposition, a state of emergency, the banning of strikes, army manning of public utilities and essential services, the distribution of food within factories to induce a return to work; the presence of four serving army generals in the

Polish government, including Premier Jaruzelski, makes this even more credible. But in the first year since August 1980 not a single shot has been fired in anger in Poland, and internal repressions cannot be expected to materialise lightly. The latest developments (August 1981) indicate a newly found restraint on the part of Union leaders and willingness to negotiate on both sides; there are still reasonable grounds for sober optimism.

III Conclusions

The Polish crisis is systemic, i.e. deeply rooted in the economic and political processes of Polish society as a socialist system. Imbalances built into the centrally planned economy (such as its excesssive propensity to accumulate, which frustrated attempts at economic reform), and the centralisation of political power associated with it, have combined with adverse exogenous factors (natural and international) to produce a crisis of exceptional depth and duration.

Polish official writings view the crisis as a consequence of 'deformations' of the socialist system due to departures from the established principles of socialist planning and management. 'Summing up the assessment of the causes of the present crisis in our country it is necessary to stress that they do not derive from the systemic principles of the socialist economy but, on the contrary, from the violation of those principles, the failure to observe objective regularities, the underestimation of economic laws as well as the lack of use of the possibilities created by the socialist system, and in particular by the socialist planned economy' ('Raport', 1981, pp. 38–9; see also Pajestka, 1981).

The example of other 'socialist countries operating in conditions similar to ours, such as Czechoslovakia, the GDR and Hungary, which succeeded in utilising better the possibilities of the socialist system, avoided crisis and succeeded in achieving more favourable indicators of economic growth and a more harmonic and balanced development of the economy' is given. The 'Raport' concludes 'the fundamental guarantee for reestablishing the development of our economy, interrupted by the present crisis, is a return to the principles of the socialist economy' (p. 39). Brezhnev's letter of 5 June, addressed to the Central Committee of the PZPR on behalf of the Soviet CP Central Committee, also refers unspecified to 'serious errors resulting from the contravention of the rules of socialist construction' in Poland (Brezhnev, 1981). The 'Raport' refers more specifically to the taking of crucial strategic decisions by single individuals in spite of an appearance of collective legality, the incompetence of decision-makers, the forcing of economic decisions by 'faits-accomplis' illegalities and the inadequacy of the management system's response to the high level of education, social consciousness and rising aspirations to participation reached by the Polish working class and the entire society ('Raport', 1981, pp. 33–5).

But these 'departures' are linked to well established principles of Soviet-type socialism extant in Poland throughout the period in question. The leadership's protection from effective criticism and checks stems from democratic centralism as actually practised in the Soviet Union and East European countries and the prohibition on factionalism prevailing since 1921 in the Soviet party and adopted by other communist parties throughout the world; the incompetence of decision-makers stems from the Soviet-type 'nomenklatura'; the failure to encompass the social consciousness and aspirations of the population stems from the generalised demotion of unions and Parliament and the lack of workers' self-management which are also typical of the Soviet-type system.

To say that the Polish crisis derives from departures from the socialist system *as theorised and practised in the Soviet Union* cannot be right, indeed the only departures from *that* system observable in Poland are the recent moves towards 'socialist renewal'; accountability of party officials and delegates, wide-ranging discussions, multiple choice and secret ballot elections. If the Polish crisis derives from departures from *an ideal socialist system* then the rest of the socialist commonwealth is as vulnerable to the same kind of crisis, under similar exogenous circumstances; by the same token as often argued in conservative circles, the deep troubles of the capitalist system can be attributed to 'departures' from the perfectly competitive, friction-free ideal model, such as monopolies and unions – the crucial question is: can we have the system without the 'departures'? Recent developments within the Polish party cannot be seen as revisionism, for they move towards a socialist ideal – unless they are seen merely as an indication of the state's weakness in the face of a revolutionary challenge.

The Polish upheavals in the first twelve months since August 1980 have been widely regarded as a 'revolution' (or 'counter-revolution', according to standpoint), from 'The Times' to 'Pravda', from Leszek Kolakowski to Leonid Brezhnev. A revolution involves a sudden, drastic change in the institutions and policies of government and in personnel: if change is not sudden and drastic it is evolution; if only personnel changes it is either a coup or normal succession; if only government institutions change it is a straightforward constitutional change.

Since August 1980 there have been sudden and drastic personnel changes: the First Secretary, two Premiers (three since early 1980), 90 per cent of Party Congress delegates, 90 per cent of Central Committee members, three quarters of the Politbureau, hundreds of regional officers, government officials and enterprise managers. There have also been sudden changes in institutions of government (or conditioning government power): a 10-million strong Solidarity Union, Rural Solidarity, over one thousand self-management organs, new groupings and associations, as well as the moves towards 'socialist renewal' reviewed above.

But while the changes within the Party are unprecedented, they have altered only procedures and policies, without changing ideology, systemic commitments, or the pattern of international alliances. The new institutions outside the Party are parallel to, not substitutes for the Party (or even the older Unions), as witnessed by dual membership of both Party and Solidarity by a million people; they have succeeded in changing some Party and government policies, but have not asserted themselves as a substitute for the Party. The eventual identity assumed by the new Union does not determine whether this is a revolution: if Solidarity turns into a Western-type Union, this will simply restrict the range of government policy options; similar restrictions would derive from Solidarity acting as a de-facto political party, or joining a government coalition in a minority; if Solidarity turns into what the official union should have been, a partner in government from outside, expressing effectively working class feelings and aspirations, it brings the Polish system closer to the socialist ideal; if it simply continues to move between these roles the pressure for party 'renewal' will continue; but the militancy of the new institutions cannot be stepped up without economic ruin and the breakdown of law and order, leading to an authoritarian solution before the new institutions have a chance of substantiating their access to power.

The year of intensive change in after-August 1980 Poland has brought about a 'cultural' revolution; a change in attitudes towards authority, an expression of pent-up aspirations, a change in generational balance of power, demands for participation in decision-making at all levels and the assertion of individual liberties. If these developments are consolidated, Poland will have produced an improved brand of socialism and reduced the chance of a similar crisis repeating itself. Other socialist countries, however, are unlikely to be seriously affected by either the Polish economic crisis or its political developments.

Polish political trends are deeply rooted in the specific national features discussed above and strictly dependent on the scale and depth of the economic crisis experienced by Poland. There are no automatic transmission mechanisms of political change apart from minor measures such as generalised attempts at revamping the old unions. On the contrary, automatic reactions are more likely to take the form of pre-emptive measures, such as the Czech firm clampdown on dissent, and the widespread curbs on travel contacts with Poland. Process of Party renewal and union reform cannot be ruled out, but would have to be home-based and home-made.

There are some transmission mechanisms for economic crisis within the socialist commonwealth: the burden for Eastern Europe and especially the Soviet Union for aid and credits extended to Poland; the disruption caused by the Polish failure to honour commitments to Comecon, especially for coal deliveries; the lower contribution that Poland can now be expected to make to the development of natural resources within Comecon and to defence. But given the relative size of Poland and its socialist partners, the Polish crisis – though a drag on resources – cannot be transmitted on anything like the Polish scale.

However, the same kind of symptoms experienced by Poland have been present in the Soviet and East European economies since the mid-1970s and there is a systemic predisposition to economic crisis:

(i) economic growth has slowed down throughout the area, especially in the Soviet Union, Czechoslovakia and Hungary; Bulgaria is the only exception. Actual decline has been recorded in important sectors in some years (see for instance Marer, 1980); growth targets in current plans acknowledge this trend;

(ii) agricultural output throughout Eastern Europe which, in the decade to 1973 rose by 5 per cent a year, slowed down to 3 per cent in the following five years, fell in 1979 and recovered only slightly in 1980;

(iii) external indebtedness for the seven European members of Comecon rose from $8.4 billion in 1971 to $64.7 billion in 1979 (Portes, 1981); the per-capita burden of foreign debt in 1979 was greater for Hungary (at $702 per head) than for Poland (at $568 per head; see Maciejewski, 1981); according to IMF trade projections, the current account deficit of the East European balance of payments in 1981 is expected to be almost double the 1979 level and $1.6 billion greater than the 1980 level at $6.2 billion ('The Times', 20 July 1981);

(iv) with the exception of Poland and the Soviet Union, terms of trade for East European countries have deteriorated over the 1970s and the trend is continuing (Marer, 1980);

(v) in the late 1970s open inflation has crept up throughout the area, outside the Soviet Union; shortages of basic consumption goods persist and their effect is becoming cumulative, successive inflationary 'gaps' raising the inflationary 'overhand';

(vi) there are recent signs of unemployment of capital (for instance in Czechoslovakia) due to structural problems and shortages of imported inputs;

(vii) inefficiency in the use of productive factors is increasingly reported and leads to pressure for economic reform; the burden of inefficiency has been made greater by the energy crisis, since consumption of energy per unit of output in Eastern Europe is twice the West European level (the share of total energy from domestic sources is falling throughout the area, even for surplus countries such as Poland — until recently — and the Soviet Union).

It is widely accepted that this deterioration in economic performance to a large extent is due to the exhaustion of 'extensive' sources of economic growth, i.e. to the increasingly biting constraints of labour and natural resources supply, and to the unsuitability of the centralised Soviet-type model of resource allocation to the 'intensive' stage of growth now reached by these economies; hence the widespread attempt at economic reform throughout the area to raise economic efficiency. But, just as in Poland, the shortages and excess demand caused by over-ambitious policies of accumulation and growth have led to either postponement or failure of economic reform. The only apparent exception has been Hungary in the last decade, but there are now signs of reversion to the traditional model (Hare, 1981). The alteration of phases of economic and/or political decentralisation, and phases of reversals, seems a general feature of socialist development (for an attempt to construct a model of such an economic/political cycle, see Nuti, 1979).

Socialist countries outside Poland are subject to the same systemic mechanism of economic and political fluctuations, capable of generating a crisis. Czechoslovakia (where the high level of industrial development clashes most with the system of economic management) and Romania (where a rigid party structure and personality cult are close to earlier Polish conditions) would probably rate the shortest odds. But disequilibrium in consumption markets and industrial disorganisation are still at trivial levels compared with Poland; the exogenous factors — especially international ones — that have so greatly contributed to the Polish crisis have already been absorbed by other socialist countries and are unlikely to recur in the short and medium run, compounding domestic troubles; a considerable switch of resources to agriculture and consumption industries is in progress in the current plans. On 12 August 1981 a joint statement by the Central Committee and the Council of Ministers announced a fresh Soviet commitment to 'providing more and better consumer goods'; Hungary has already shortened the working week. A lesson will have been learned from the Polish crisis about the importance of responding to popular consciousness and demands. In the 1980s the other socialist countries are more likely to suffer temporary economic stagnation than the dramatic decline and disruption recorded in Poland.

Postscript (March 1982)

The critical state of the Polish economy, which had given Solidarity a powerful political lever and Jaruzelski a plausible pretext for military rule, continues to affect the course of Polish events. The Military Council of National Salvation has already taken those unpopular austerity measures — formerly tenaciously obstructed by the new political and trade union movement — which are indispensable for economic recovery: a return to a 42-hour 6-day working week, the reduction of rations, and above all a drastic increase in the price of consumption goods, particularly foodstuffs and heating. The Military have also gone ahead with partial reform of the system of industrial organisation and planning, implementing those parts of the reform project which did not clash with military rule, such as dissolving large associations of enterprises operating in the same sector (but suspending self-management for the time being). In spite of the return to work and the end of strikes, however, these measures on their own are not sufficient to achieve economic reconstruction and recovery. The reopening of negotiations with elected workers' representatives and the achievement of some kind of political-economic compromise — desirable per se — are an essential precondition in order to avoid passive resistance in factories, normalise agricultural supplies and reactivate trade and financial links with the West. For a change, economic constraints can play a positive role.

In 1981 national income in Poland fell by 15 per cent, i.e. back to the 1974 level. Money wages rose 25 per cent, and so did prices, but consumption supplies fell by 10 per cent, leading to a further increase in the already large amount of unspendable cash in the hands of the population, not matched by goods in the shops. Industrial output fell by 13 per cent, back to the 1976 level; agricultural output rose by 4 per cent with respect to 1980, but this was a bad year, and this important sector was back to the 1972 level; besides, food procurements by the state slumped (meat by 25 per cent). Martial law has worsened this picture, by reducing both industrial production (because of passive resistance, shortage of imported materials and sheer disorganisation of the planning system) and the marketing of foodstuffs.

Already in 1981 the suspension of investment programmes, lack of energy, raw materials and imported goods, had generated a labour surplus in some industries (building, machinery, metallurgy), exacerbated by attempts at rationalisation. At the same time, labour shortages prevailed in mining and agriculture. The Planning Commission envisaged the redeployment of 175 thousand workers in 1981, 262 thousand in 1982, 223 thousand in 1983, and Labour Minister Antoni Rajkiewicz indicated that in the near future 180 thousand workers would have been dismissed from industrial enterprises, 150 thousand from the building industry and 60 thousand from transport. It was expected that 90,000 new entrants into the labour market would not have found a job. The presence of a substantial labour surplus — which economists put at over one million people — was also revealed by measures for early retirement, part-time labour, and generous incentives for transferring to the private sector. At the same time productive capacity was underutilised by 30–35 per cent, with peaks of over 50 per cent, so that capital was also 'unemployed' because of structural problems and the lack of imported goods (from steel cans to distilled water, and not only advanced technology) on which Poland had become exceedingly dependent.

Polish external debt, by the end of 1981, had reached 25.5 billion dollars with Western banks and governments, plus 4.7 billion dollars with the socialist bloc. This is no more than 1 per cent of the value of Polish established coal reserves (if they were dug out of the ground and transported to Hamburg — a big if), or two-year cost of unemployment in Britain at the present rate; it was also, however, an amount substantially greater than the whole reserves of the Bank of England, and more than twice the level of debt that the Polish economy could cope with in normal conditions. In the actual conditions Poland not only could not repay debt as it matured but could not even pay all interests. On 26 March 1981 Poland stopped repayment of maturing debt and the amounts still outstanding were rescheduled for repayment over eight years with a four year grace period, but this arrangement was

conditional on Poland paying up 500 million dollars overdue interest
still outstanding, before the end of 1981; another 800 million dollars
were still owing to Western governments for 1981. Polish gold and hard
currency reserves, on the other hand, stood at a miserly 228 million
dollars. (Of those 500 million dollars overdue interest, 200 million were
paid around the end of the year after military rule, apparently out of
Soviet aid; Poland has promised to pay up the remaining 300 millions
by mid-February.) Another 6.5 billion dollars are maturing in 1982,
plus another 3 billion interest; Poland needs to reschedule these matur-
ities as well, and find fresh funds for paying interest. Trade balance
with the West was reached at the end of 1981, but at the cost of a 30
per cent fall in imports from the West, and parallel fall in industrial
output and income. The external constraint, and above all the loss,
in the course of 1981, of at least 1.5 billion dollars of short term loans
not renewed by Western bankers, is the major cause of the Polish
economic collapse in 1981. By withdrawing short term support,
bankers have behaved wisely from their individual viewpoint, but
collectively they have undermined the viability of their debtor and
damaged their own collective interest.

External imbalance was accompanied by an enormous internal
imbalance, under the guise of open inflation (10 per cent in 1980 and
25 per cent in 1981) but above all of 'repressed' inflation, i.e. endemic
shortages of consumption goods, including necessities, rationing (which
however was not covered by supplies, and therefore coexisted with
queues and inflation) and hyperinflation in the black market. US dollars,
officially worth 33.5 zlotys until the end of 1981, in the black market
had reached 15 times their official value. Already in the autumn there
was literally nothing at all in the shops; the population would buy
immediately at unrealistically low prices anything put on the market,
and would redistribute it through barter, while the national currency
was replaced as a unit of account, means of payment and store of value,
by foreign currency, cigarettes, alcohol. By the end of the year the
population held over 1,000 billion zlotys in liquid assets of which only
a small fraction was voluntarily held; the rest was simply unspendable,
and corresponded — at the official exchange rate — to the level of
external debt. There can be no doubt that the wage increases obtained
at Gdansk in August 1980, raising incomes by a third while consumption supply fell by 20 per cent in sixteen months, had caused directly
the total disruption of consumption markets. Gross profits had
fallen to zero in the socialised sector over the first three quarters
of 1981. No more than two thirds of current incomes were covered by

consumption goods, and the deficit was cumulated at a fast rate. Strikes and labour unrest cannot have done much damage: according to official sources 10,500,000 working hours were lost in 1981 through strikes, i.e. less than an hour per worker per year; even if hours lost had been ten times as great, output could not have suffered much. But the free Saturday and the reduction of the working week, which had caused a fall by 7.5 per cent in hours worked, must have had a deleterious effect on the state of supplies, directly and through its effect on coal output and exports.

In this situation, the systematic refusal by Solidarity to accept austerity measures and price increases, and the government inability to go ahead without Solidarity's consent, had given great power to the new movement. The relentless and continued use of this power, however, threatened not only the system but the state itself. The economic measures taken by the military government had been prepared and discussed for at least six months, and some (like the devaluation of the zloty and the increase in the price of industrial inputs) had been announced long beforehand. The price increases decreed on 1 February — by 241 per cent on food and 171 per cent on heating — appear exorbitant but, apart from being partly compensated by compensatory wage increases and the revaluation of savings, one should remember that as long as consumption supplies are maintained, even large price increases do not imply a fall in the standard of living, when there is a large unsatisfied demand before the increase. The new prices simply correspond to the harsh reality of Polish consumption supplies. The price increases are a step in the right direction.

Economic recovery, however, cannot be achieved by military decree. The military can force the return to work by coercion or by positive inducement — such as the distribution of clothing and food at the place of work — but are completely powerless against workers' passive resistance in factories. Absenteeism, sabotage, obstructionism, the Italian-style 'refusal to work' can still worsen further the economic situation, prolong and harden the state of emergency, which in turn would inflict new economic losses through economic sanctions. The suspension of self-management is also economically damaging, not so much because self-management might improve efficiency but because it was always understood, in negotiations with Solidarity, that this could be the political counterpart of economic austerity. Peasants are also beyond the reach of the military; barring requisition, which would destroy future prospects of food supply, peasants cannot be forced to feed the towns, and indeed the possibility of bread shortages in the spring looms large for Polish consumers.

No matter how strong and reliable the Polish army and security forces may be, ultimately Polish generals are in the hand of Polish miners and workers, and Western bankers and governments. The plan for 1982 — now set aside — contained a pessimistic version and an optimistic one according to assumptions about coal output and trade with the West. The difference between 175 and 155 million tons of coal output (against 203 million in 1979 and 163 million in 1981), and between balanced trade with the West or the necessity of running a 1.2 billion dollar surplus, in the 1982 plan implies a difference between +2.2 per cent growth or −8.3 per cent decline in income produced, and an even stronger difference in income distributed (respectively −1 and −15.6 per cent). Thus it is imperative for the military to come to an accommodation, to a compromise which would enjoy a minimum degree of popular consensus necessary to persuade miners to dig coal, peasants to sow, and Western governments and bankers to continue with aid trade and loans. Otherwise the shortage of coal for power stations and exports, food shortages, the lack of imported materials and semi-finished products, in the course of a few months will precipitate an economic crisis of such proportions as to unleash popular protest and revolt of a type familiar with Northern Ireland or El Salvador, in which case there is no doubt that Warsaw Pact troops would intervene.

Polish workers and military men, and Western bankers and governments are playing the last hand of a dangerous game in which either they all win, in which case an economic recovery can still take place, western credits are protected and at least part of the political achievements of the after-August can be preserved; or they all lose, with Poland starving under Soviet occupation, Western financial circles are disrupted by the write-off of Polish debt, American Mid-West farmers lose markets, Western firms lose sales of gas equipment and access to Soviet gas. The lesson of Poland's 'state of war' is that intransigence does not pay; unfortunately, there is still no sign that that lesson has been learned by the protagonists of this painful story, in Poland and outside.

Acknowledgements

The preparation of this essay has benefited greatly from three visits to Poland in May–June and November 1980 and July 1981, respectively as a guest of Lodz University, the Polish Economic Association and the University of Warsaw, which have given me the opportunity to collect research materials and talk to colleagues, government and union officials. I have also discussed various parts of this essay at seminars in the Universities of Birmingham, South Wales, Leeds, Hull, Oxford, Warwick, and the LSE.

Note

* An earlier version of this paper was published in 'Socialist Register', November 1981.

References

AEW (Akademia Ekonomiczna we Wroclawiu), 1981, Propozycje zmian w systemie funkcjonowania gospodarki, 'Zycie Gospodarcze', no. 2, 11 January

Balcerowicz, L. et al., 1980, 'Alternatywy rozwoju, reforma gospodarcza — glowne kierunki i sposoby realizacji', PTE, Warsaw

Brezhnev, L., 1981. Letter of 5 June from the Central Committee of the Soviet Communist Party to the Central Committee of the PZPR, 'Financial Times', 11 June

Bromke, A., 1981, Poland's upheaval — an interim report, 'The World Today', June

Brus, W. 1980, Lessons of the Polish Summer, 'Marxism Today', November

'East-West', 1981, 'Poland, the current crisis and outlook', Brussels

EUI (Economic Intelligence Unit), 1981, 'Quarterly Economic Review of Poland, East Germany', nos. 2 and 3, London

Hare P.G., Radice H.K., Swain N., 1981, 'Hungary: a decade of economic reform'

IKCHZ (Instytut Koniunktur i Cen Handlu Zagranicznego), 1980, 'Main indicators of Polish foreign trade development', Warsaw

Jozefiak, C., 1981, Votum separatum, 'Polityka', no. 8, 21 February

Kalecki, M., 1969, 'Introduction to the theory of growth of the socialist economy', Blackwell, London

Kolankiewicz, G., 1981, The politics of 'socialist renewal', unpublished paper presented to the annual conference of the British National Association for Soviet and East European Studies, Cambridge 21–3 March

KPZdsRG (Komisja Partyjno-Rzadowa do spraw Reformy Gospodarczej), 1981 (a), 'Podstawowe zalozenia reformy gospodarczej — Projekt', KiW, Warsaw

KPZdsRG (Komisja Partyjno-Rzadowa do spraw Reformy Gospodarczej), 1981 (b) 'Kierunki reformy gospodarczej — Projekt; Projekty ustaw o przedsiebiorst-wach panstwowych, — o samorzadzie przedsiebiorstwa panstwowego', Nakladem Trybuny Ludu, July

Kotowicz-Jawor J., 1979, Presja inwestycyjna w rozwoju gospodarczym, 'Gospodarka Planowa', no. 3

Kramer, L., 1981, Proba analizy porownawczej, 'Zycie Gospodarcze', no. 12, 22 March

Maciejewski, W., 1981, Europejskie kraje RWPG w pierwszej polowie lat osiem-dziesiatych, 'Wektory' no. 1 (forthcoming)

'Maly Rocznik Statystyczny', 1981, GUS, Warsaw

Marer, P., 1980, Economic performance and prospects in Eastern Europe;

analytical summary and interpretation of findings (mimeo)

Moskwa, A. et al., 1981, 'Alternatywy rozwoju — Kierunki reform politiyczno-gospodarczych w Polsce'. PTE, Warsaw

NOT (Naczelna Organizacja Techniczna), 1981

Nuti, D.M., 1977, Large corporations and the reform of Polish industry, 'Jahrbuch der Wirtschaft Osteuropas', Vol. 7, Munich

Nuti, D.M., 1979, The contradiction of socialist economies — a Marxian interpretation, 'The Socialist Register', Merlin Press, London

Nuti, D.M., 1981, Industrial enterprises in Polish industry, 1973–80: economic policies and reforms, and Postscript on Poland, in I. Jeffries (ed.), 'The industrial enterprise in Eastern Europe', Praeger

Pajestka, J., 1981, 'Polski kryzys lat 1980–1981', KiW, Warsaw

Pelczynski, Z.A., 1981, Stalemate and after in Poland, 'New Society', 5 February

Portes, R., 1977, The control of inflation — lessons from East European experience, 'Economica', n. 2

Portes, R., 1981, 'The Polish crisis: Western economic policy options', RIIA, London

Program ('Rzadowy program przezwyciezania kryzysu oraz stabilizowania gospodarki kraju'), 1981, Nakladem Trybuny Ludu, Warsaw, July

Protokoly ('Protokoly porozumien Gdansk Szczecin Jastrzebie — Statut NSZZ Solidarnosc'), 1980, KAW, Warsaw

PTE (Polskie Towarzystwo Ekonomiczne), 1980, 'Propozycje Zasadniczych Rozwiazan Reformy Gospodarczej w Polsce', Warsaw

Raport ('Rzadowy raport o stanie gospodarki'), 1981, Nakladem Trybuny Ludu, Warsaw, July

'Rocznik Statystyczny', 1980, GUS, Warsaw

Sadowski, W. — Herer, W., 1981, Nawis inflacyjny (mimeo), Warsaw (forthcoming in 'Ekonomista')

'Siec', 1981, 'Projekt ustawy o przedsiebiorstwie spolecznym', Warsaw

Simarupang B., 1981, 'Polish agriculture in the 1970s; Some problems', Research Memorandum no. 8110, University of Amsterdam

Staniszkis J., 1981, Poland in the 1980, unpublished paper presented in the Annual Conference of the British Association of Soviet and East European Studies, Cambridge, 21–3 March

Szafar T., 1979, Contemporary political opposition in Poland (mimeo, unpublished) Harvard University

Uchwala Rady Ministrów nr. 118/80 z dnia 17 listopada 1980 w sprawie zmian w systemie kierowania przedsiebiorstwami państwowymi w 1981. 1981, 'Zycie Gospodarcze', nr. 3

2 THE POLISH CRISIS: WILL IT SPREAD AND WHAT WILL BE THE OUTCOME?

Stanislaw Gomulka

Introduction

The fact that economic difficulties, while very considerable among all the Comecon countries, have assumed (so far) the truly crisis proportions only in Poland, may be interpreted to indicate that not the common systemic factors but the specific macroeconomic policies and decisions of the Polish government have been at fault. There are good grounds to think, however, that this would be too narrow a view to take. While the modernisation and industrialisation processes have been comparatively fast in the USSR and Eastern Europe, this commendable success seems to have brought about new serious economic and social problems all over the area. Although these problems may be thought to be the by-products of success, they are of the kind which the highly centralised political and economic institutions, developed originally for the purpose of conducting rapid industrialisation in a peasant-dominated society under hostile political conditions, appear now to be singularly ill-suited to solve. Thus, and this is the key thesis to be developed in this paper, events in Poland may well be an indication of things to come in other centrally planned economies as well, although their own crises need not be as acute and politically far reaching as the one in Poland.

Poland in the years 1976–81 was a case of social laboratory at work, demonstrating vividly how major economic problems breed mass political unrest which, then, helps to spread dissenting ideas and promotes new opinion leaders who, in turn, attempt to channel this unrest into social pressures for immediate policy changes and longer term institutional reforms. But the rise of Solidarity has clearly put at risk the stability and the very survival of the traditional communist system. The threat of political democratisation to the communist rule, in particular Solidarity's insistence on free elections to Polish Parliament, was real enough. So it had to be removed. The military takeover was, in this sense, the system's act of self-defence, even if desperate and crude.

Following the takeover, the communist elite under Jaruzelski's leadership seems still ready to identify and gradually introduce those

65

economic and political reforms that might be thought capable of meeting the main economic problems without, at the same time, putting at any serious risk the elite's nearly absolute power. Since the beginning of 1982 an attempt is being made to amend the traditional system by combining what is intended to be, eventually, a far-reaching marketisation of the economy with some ideological flexibility and ruthless control in the political and culture domains. This thus appears to be a variant of the Hungarian model which, I shall suggest, is likely to be a serious contender for adoption by other East European countries if and when their own difficulties assume crisis proportions.

Systemic Factors in Poland's Economic Crisis

The key to understanding the events of the 1970s is no doubt the development of large macroeconomic imbalances, both internal (excess of aggregate demand for consumer goods) and external (foreign debt). The reasons for the failure of the government to keep the two imbalances within 'safe limits' are many and I discuss them elsewhere more fully (Gomulka, 1982a). But the principal reasons are few and worth noting for their systemic nature.

The origin of the internal imbalance can be traced directly to the worker uprising of December 1970. That event not only forced a change of government, but, significantly, in exchange for industrial peace the workers won also a freeze on food prices at the pre-December level and a promise of fast increases in real wages. The government's freedom to set prices and wages at whatever levels are deemed appropriate — a vital instrument of central planning — was thus partly lost. (An unsuccessful bid to regain this control was to be made in June 1976 and in the summer of 1980.) This loss of control, though partial, had probably the effect of prompting the new government to use outside resources in larger measure than would have otherwise been the case for investment and consumption purposes. The much increased credit imports produced an economic boom in the early 1970s, and this in turn raised the workers expectations of fast and sustained improvement in their standard of living. Secondly, the wave of machinery and technology imports in the years 1972–6 stimulated imports of materials, components and parts. At the same time the share of exports in total industrial output failed to increase, rendering the government export plans wildly optimistic. The unreformed economy was behaving in a manner which many economists had expected it would. In particular, manufacturing firms were quite happy to increase dollar imports but were unable or unwilling to increase dollar exports. Thirdly, Poland in the 2nd half of the 1970s became a major net importer of food. This event appears to be a part of a general pattern. Like most less-developed countries, Poland in the 1950s and the 1960s had a sizeable trade surplus in agricultural products and minerals. That surplus was used to pay for net imports of 'technology-intensive' goods. However, with the progress of industrialisation the domestic market for food and minerals increased fast. Two systemic factors have accentuated this trend. One was that the choice of techniques and innovations tend to be heavily biased towards a high material intensiveness, with a consequent high consumption of energy, steel, cement and so forth per unit of value added, and a corresponding bias in the composition of investment outlays in favour of sectors producing these inputs. For example, in 1979 the consumption of energy per dollar of national product was (in coal equivalent) 0.48kg in Japan, 0.56kg in West Germany, 0.6kg in Austria, 0.89kg in the UK, but 1.5kg in Poland (Jerzy Kleer, 'Polityka', 13 March 1982: the UK's high figure may be due to the use of official exchange rates which probably significantly undervalued the UK's national income in that particular year). The other systemic factor relates to the apparently increasing bargaining power of industrial workers as they became more numerous and more sophisticated. In contrast to market economies, where the responsibility for price increases is widely diffused, in centrally planned economies this responsibility rests solely with the government. Consequently, price increases, especially when they come in bunches and jumps, tend to unite the workers against the government. The authorities in the USSR and Eastern Europe appear to be aware that their price decisions send shock waves among the consumers and that the possibility of workers' active resistance may well be increasing as industrialisation and modernisation proceeds. Guided by this perception, the authorities seem to be increasingly more reluctant to impose such price rises for basic consumer goods that would be required to maintain both market equilibria at home and a sizeable surplus for export. This reluctance was particularly in evidence in Poland, but also in the USSR, the two countries becoming, in the 1970s, net food importers on a large scale. (In Poland, the trade imbalance in food products represented, at $4.3 bn, 24.4 per cent of the total dollar trade imbalance for the decade.)

New Causes of Slower Economic Growth in the USSR and E. Europe

The system of economic and political institutions in Poland was, in the 1970s, quite similar to that prevailing in the other (developed) Comecon countries, among which only Hungary is something of an exception. It is well known that under such a system market competitiveness and financial discipline are low and allocative inefficiencies are large and widespread. Moreover, enterprises tend to resist innovation, especially material-saving and quality enhancing innovation. Low price and quantity flexibilities result in persistent micro-disequilibria: shortages of some goods and surpluses of others. But these important systemic deficiencies are not new, and yet there are grounds to think that the system had served the USSR and Eastern Europe relatively well until, say, the mid 1970s. The growth slowdown in Soviet industry is admittedly not new either, having been a post-1947 phenomenon. This long term slowdown may be explained however by reference to two transitory influences, the powerful initially, but weakening over time, positive effect on industrial growth of the post-war economic recovery, and, second, the gradual exhaustion of the agricultural labour surplus as a source of industrial employment growth (see Gomulka, 1977, for details). The recent economic difficulties appear to have qualitatively different causes. What are these causes?

Clearly, apart from the agricultural labour surplus, it was also the accumulated technology of the more developed West that in the past represented a major growth reserve of the centrally planned economies (CPEs). This reserve has been partly activated already, contributing to the productivity and output growth in the past. (For an estimate of the contribution of variation in technological gaps to the variation in productivity growth rates see Gomulka (1982b).) The point is that although the technological gaps that remain are still considerable in most industries, the innovative capabilities of the present Soviet system may well be such as to prevent the industrially advanced CPEs from making significant further gains in closing the gaps. This interpretation is consistent with the notion that the asymptotic, or equilibrium, relative technological gaps are system (as well as culture) specific and that the actual gaps are now close to such equilibrium levels.

The interpretation must also be seen in conjunction with the earlier analysis of how the successes in industrialisation have led to shortages in food and raw materials. We noted that it is in these kinds of goods that the region as a whole has traditionally had to earn a surplus in order to pay for technological imports. These shortages represent now a serious constraint because the region's sales of other goods continue to be marginal. This balance-of-payments constraint to growth is looming large for the whole Soviet bloc. It is becoming particularly binding for the East European economies which, in contrast to the USSR, have neither the minerals needed to obtain Western technology nor R & D resources for effective inventive and imitative activity at home.

Another powerful factor that had been a growth reserve in the past but now acts to decelerate growth is the policy, pursued by all the CPEs until recently, of concentrating investment in industry at the expense of infrastructure. The policy was quite wise as long as the infrastructure was not fully utilised. But this appears to be no longer the case. In particular the transport and communication sectors are widely acknowledged to represent new serious bottlenecks.

Incidentally, these two sectors, along with other underinvested sectors, such as housing, agriculture and water supplies, happen to be highly capital-intensive. Consequently, when these non-industrial sectors began to attract, as they must, a much greater share of investment resources than they have in the past, a fall in the aggregate productivity of capital will follow.

Soviet System in Search of a Suitable Response: the Alternatives

The Soviet system has been clearly instrumental in the past in raising fast both the rate of accumulation and the rate of labour participation, the key extensive factors of growth. But the failure of the import-led strategy of growth in Eastern Europe and the military takeover in Poland appear to indicate forcefully that the system has serious flaws in that it restricts or prevents desirable qualitative changes, crucial among which are technological innovation and political democratisation. I have noted above that in the past these flaws were of lesser significance for economic growth and social stability than they are now, and that the difference is especially marked for the group of small East European countries.

In the area of innovation these countries are faced now with what must be for their communist elites a disturbing dilemma: they must either sharply increase the allocative role of markets and competition at home, probably at the expense of some long-standing socialist objectives, such as job security, or else sharply reduce technological imports from the West and accept their present technological inferiority as something more or less permanent. The urgent need to restrain the large dollar debt from rising still further must give this dilemma an added emphasis, as must the prospect of having to increase imports of oil from the dollar market in the course of the 1980s and beyond.

In the political domain, the centre's ability to control fully consumer prices and workers' wages is under strain. The Polish crisis suggests that the pressure is probably building up either to broaden the narrow political base of present governments, so that their decisions concerning prices and wages, as well as other matters, may be seen by individual workers to command legitimacy or, alternatively, to replace command central planning by a competitive market mechanism, so that the responsibility for price and wage changes is diffused.

The long story of reforms in Eastern Europe suggests that major reforms are likely to be adopted only under the weight of a serious crisis. (Hungary is probably something of an exception, although the reform there is not really radical, the state retaining some of the key instruments of direct influence: managerial appointments, funding most large and medium investment projects, foreign exchange allocation, and fairly strict prices and wages controls.) The key ingredients for such crisis appear now present in the whole of Eastern Europe, since faced with a net debt of about $65 bn and a continuing balance of payments deficit of some $10 bn per annum, the region is being forced to curtail severely its dollar imports, industrial outputs and investment activity.

The response of the Polish communist elite to the crisis may well be indicative of the kind of systemic changes that may be adopted throughout the region. If one overlooks the ideological content of the state propaganda and the question of ownership of the productive assets, the system towards which Eastern Europe seems to be moving would be similar to that prevailing in Spain under Franco, in Greece under the colonels or in Germany under Hitler, with comparative freedom in the economic domain but strict control in any other field being its essential features. The level of repression, actual and potential, needed to sustain such a system in a modern and well educated society may have to be high, however. This must be so especially in Poland where an inevitable further large decline in national product in 1982, expected by the Polish government to be some 9–10 per cent, is likely to be followed by a period of slow recovery, high unemployment and high inflation at a very low level of per capita consumption. Moreover, Poland's certain inability to pay interest for a number of years introduces an element of uncertainty in East-West economic relations, since now Poland may be declared, or choose herself to declare, to be in default at any time. Poland's default would in turn represent a shock that may trigger off severe credit restrictions for the whole of Eastern Europe, and hence increase the risk of further defaults. Should such a chain reaction actually come about, some of the countries may also follow Poland in adopting a mixed economic system that would combine some decentralisation and marketisation with a degree of militarisation, the latter to be retained until the economic slide is stopped and the Comecon Group converted to a more self-dependent economic entity.

References

Fallenbuchl, Zbigniew, M., 1982, Poland: A Way Out?, mimeo, February

Fallenbuchl, Zbigniew, M., 1982, The Polish Economic Crisis, mimeo, February

Gomulka, Stanislaw, 1977, Slowdown in Soviet Industrial Growth 1947–1975 Reconsidered, 'European Economic Review', 10, 37–49

Gomulka, Stanislaw, 1982a, Macroeconomic Reserves, Constraints and Systemic Factors in the Dynamics of the Polish Crisis 1980–82, 'Jahrbuch der Wirtschaft Osteuropas', March

Gomulka, Stanislaw, 1982b, Industrialisation and the Rate of Growth: Eastern Europe 1955–1975, mimeo, forthcoming in the 'Journal of Post-Keynesian Economics'

3 THE ANATOMY OF ECONOMIC FAILURE IN SOVIET-TYPE SYSTEMS

Jan Drewnowski

Inability to Perform and/or to Reform is a Fact for which no Explanation is Found in Economic Theory

The inefficiency of centrally planned economies is a well known fact. In terms of national product per head, productivity of labour and levels of living even the most advanced centrally planned economies lag behind the advanced market economies. All efforts to 'overtake and surpass' capitalism have failed dismally and the accomplishment of this objective seems to be as remote as ever.

Those responsible for economic policies in centrally planned systems have been long aware of that state of affairs and they persistently proposed all sorts of changes which were supposed to improve economic performance. Since about 1955 most centrally planned economies have been subject of a sequence of reforms.[1] All in vain. Some minor corrections in the functioning of the systems were sometimes obtained but no fundamental improvement was ever brought about. For some reason the centrally planned economies proved to be neither able to perform nor to reform.[2]

This phenomenon certainly calls for an explanation. Essentially what needs to be explained are the causes of the difference in performance of the two economic systems operating in the contemporary world. A difference which is evidently rooted in some specific permanent characteristics of the systems in question.

It could be reasonably expected that the explanation of this difference should be provided by economic theory. The problem is certainly general enough and important enough to warrant this. And yet economic theory, or more precisely the theory of socialism and the theory of comparative economic systems, does not seem to be able to throw much light on the problem.

What can be inferred from contemporary mainstream economic theory seems to contradict the observed facts. It is not only difficult to find a theoretical explanation of the inefficiency of the centrally planned systems, but it is possible to argue that theoretical reasoning leads to the conclusion that centrally planned systems ought to be more efficient than market systems.

In discussing this problem it is probably proper to begin by referring to the ancient Mises-Lange argument on the feasibility of rational economic calculus under socialism.[3] Evidently if Mises were right and economic calculus impossible, that would have been a valid theoretical explanation of the inefficiency of centrally planned economies. But Mises was wrong and whatever may be the faults in Lange's approach[4] and the imperfections of the economic theory of socialism as we know it at present, it cannot be seriously contended today that economic calculus is impossible in centrally planned economies. Once this is proved it is understandable that Lange has come to the conclusion that socialism is in principle more efficient than capitalism. He has stated it explicitly in his famous essay.[5]

It is possible to enlarge upon Lange's argument and try to compare merits and demerits of the two systems in achieving efficiency and reducing all wastage of resources.

The prime source of wastage under capitalism is the existence of monopolies which prevent an optimal utilisation of resources. Wastages may be also caused by the mechanism of competition at the stage before the competitive equilibrium is reached. It is then that the unsuccessful competitors fall by the wayside, their efforts being frustrated and assets becoming unusable or greatly diminished in value.

Wastages and inefficiencies in market economies are often caused by imperfect information: entrepreneurs who are making decisions of the utmost importance for the national economy may be well informed as to their immediate surroundings, but possess no reliable information on the national or international situation and even less about its outlook for the future. They tend to take a short term view as they are not able to scan a wider time horizon. Hence come errors and contradictions in their decisions and consequent failure and waste affecting both decision making entrepreneurs and the national economy as a whole.

In centrally planned economies these causes of inefficiency do not exist. All information about the present position and prospects for the future can be made available to decision makers both at the centre and at enterprise level. Moreover, as the economy is centrally guided, many developments are easily predictable or quasi certain. Consequently forecasts may be considered to be generally more reliable. In centrally planned economies there is no inherent necessity for contradictory decisions which in capitalism are unavoidable because of the contradictory interests of decision making entrepreneurs. There is no duplication of effort resulting from competition, no wastage resulting from bankrupcies, no underutilisation of resources caused by monopolies. All in all there seems to be a good case for contending that, on theoretical grounds, a centrally planned economy can be expected to perform better than a market one.

Misguided Reforms

This lack of theoretical explanation has not prevented policy makers in centrally planned systems from realising how poor the economic performance has been, nor has it restrained them from attempts to improve it. Economic theory not being able to provide a conceptual basis for reforms, their approach has had to be pragmatic. By examining the proposed improvements it is possible to realise what in the minds of economic experts were the main causes of the notorious economic inefficiency.

The most common explanation of the inefficiency of centrally planned economies was the alleged lack of material incentives for the workers. Consequently the introduction of material incentives into the system has become the core of many reforms. They have failed very badly because they were based on fallacious reasoning.

The difference between the two systems in respect of the impact of material incentives on the productivity of labour was very greatly exaggerated. It is certain that material incentives significantly affect the productivity of small privately owned enterprises which do exist in capitalism and have no place in centrally planned economics. But this is a structural feature which is not liable to change. What is a valid subject for reforms are material incentives for workers in big enterprises. It is their productivity which is crucial for the over-all performance of the national economy. In this respect, however, centrally planned economies do not lag behind the market ones. Quite often the contrary is true. In centrally planned economies piece work pay has been much more common and many schemes for linking wages with productivity or for profit sharing have been in operation. Workers' response to those schemes has been generally disappointing and sometimes outright hostile.[6] Productivity remained constantly lower than under capitalism where such schemes do not exist and a straight daily wage is paid. It seems certain that it is not the lack of incentives which is the cause of the inefficiency and it is not by introducing them that centrally planned economies can be made efficient.

Apart from the alleged lack of incentives it is the so called 'model' of the economy which was being blamed for its poor performance. The 'model' in this context stands for the institutional setting of the economy and the rules for its functioning.

The 'institutional setting' refers to a system of institutions responsible for running the national economy. It is a hierarchical system. At the top are institutions responsible for policies on a national scale, at the bottom are units which actually perform their respective economic tasks. The system can be also divided vertically into: the planning apparatus, the financial and banking system and the system of units responsible for the production of goods and services.

Two kinds of units can be distinguished within this system of institutions: administrative units and enterprises. Enterprises may be state owned (the prevailing form), cooperative or private ones (the vanishing but sometimes tolerated form), each of these forms having their particular characteristics.

The 'rules for functioning' of the economy refer to the way the existing institutions perform their tasks and to the way they are linked with each other. Only a few of the most important problems which fall under the 'rules for functioning' can be mentioned here. First there are procedures for the preparation and implementation plans on various levels. Secondly, there is the even more general problem of centralisation and decentralisation, i.e. of the respective scope of decision-making by units at various levels. Another problem is the organisation of information flows which transmit 'inter alia' decision parameters between units operating at various levels of the hierarchical planning system. Then there is the problem of the rules for establishing these parameters. And lastly there is a question of the policy instruments through which existing markets are regulated and subordinated to the plan.

This is evidently only a very sketchy outline of what is meant by a 'model' of a centrally planned economy. It was presented here for the sole purpose of showing what were the topics of all these reforms concerned with the improvement of the 'model'.

There is no doubt that this was a legitimate subject for reforms, as it is clear that many failures in centrally planned economies can be traced to faults existing in their respective 'models'.

For many years, in a number of countries the best economic minds and the most competent organisers devoted their energies to this task. There is no doubt that some improvements were made, i.e. that the models were somewhat corrected. But it is also most remarkable that the effects of these efforts were on the whole disappointing. Very often, even when some positive results were achieved, they could not be maintained and after some time the economic performance relapsed into mediocrity.

The failure of reforms in centrally planned economies is a phenomenon which has occurred with remarkable regularity. It cannot be explained simply by the incompetence of the reformers. There are sufficient reasons to suppose that *the inefficiency of the economy has been due to causes which have escaped the attention of the economic theory and hence have been systematically overlooked by reformers.* In consequence the attempted reforms were directed either towards irrelevant changes (such as incentive systems) in which case they were bound to be ineffective, or towards relevant changes (such as model improvements) which however were never complete as some of the important causes of inefficiency were not dealt with. Consequently such reforms would have only a limited or short lived effect, as they were being frustrated by hidden faults in the system which were never affected by any reforms.

It must be admitted that the existence of at least some of such faults has not been entirely unknown to those familiar with conditions in centrally planned economies. That knowledge however has been, so to speak, kept below the threshold of analytical consciousness.[7] The problems in question were not assumed to be important enough to merit a place in theory or to become a focus of reform projects.

It is contended that this approach should be reversed: the hidden faults of the system ought to be carefully examined. It is possible that conclusions from that examination may prove highly significant for both theory and policy.

The Concept of Economic Tissue

Any theory which tries to explain the functioning of an economic system must assume that there are some rules by which all decision makers operating within the system are guided in pursuing their various activities. As those rules are obvious and never questioned, theory takes them for granted. Some may have sometimes been stated for the sake of methodological good order but were seldom discussed at all; some may have been only tacitly assumed and have never been formulated explicitly.

Just a few such assumptions can be mentioned here in order to make clear their significance. It is taken for granted that the economy operates within a definite legal system, that law and order is maintained, contracts are enforced and honesty is a prevailing practice. Moreover it is assumed that managers and professional, administrative and manual workers are able and willing to perform their respective tasks to the best of their ability. In particular it is assumed that managers are capable of collecting and evaluating information, assessing the productive capacities of their units and the impact of external factors, that they understand the directives received and exert their own judgement. In other words that they are capable and willing to make rational decisions expected of them.

Such assumptions are of course quite legitimate. It can even be said that they are an indispensable element in economic theory. They refer to what may be called the 'tissue' of the economy: to the functioning of the basic cells in the economic organism.

Assumptions about the nature of the tissue reflect our knowledge about human behaviour in respect of economic tasks, which has been acquired by observation and experience. That behaviour is in turn an outcome of cultural and economic conditions which have prevailed in society over long periods of time.

Assumptions of this kind are generalisations derived from that knowledge. They are not concerned with possible exceptions and special cases. This does not detract from their validity. The assumptions about the tissue which were enumerated above, are certainly correct in conditions which have determined the methodology and contents of economic theory as we know it at present.

Once the nature of the tissue has been assumed, theory can proceed to deal with its specific tasks without bothering further about the initial assumptions. This means that the conditions of the tissue have been taken to be a constant of no significance to the solution of the problems with which economic theory was concerned.[8]

This approach must be qualified. It is correct when, and only when, the conditions of the tissue actually remain unchanged. But this is not always necessarily so. It could be contended that the condition of the tissue is liable to change. It may improve or deteriorate and influence the performance of the economy accordingly. That means that the state of the tissue could be seen as a set of variables having an impact on the outcome of the economic process.

In what follows an attempt is made to use the tissue concept in order to explain the failure of centrally planned economies.

The Degradation of the Tissue

There seems to be enough evidence to contend that the degradation of the tissue in centrally planned economies may be the cause of their persistently disappointing performance. The exact meaning of this degradation has to be explained, its main causes discussed, its symptoms identified and its consequences examined.

The causes of the degradation have their origin in the inherent political, economic and social characteristics of the systems prevailing in countries which have adopted central planning.[9]

Suppression of Truth

The first cause of degradation is the suppression of truth. It takes the form of a deliberate policy preventing information from being available to anybody except to the selected few. This policy goes so far as to hamper the collection of information including statistical data. Secrecy is considered a virtue, openness is suspect. Disclosure of information to the unauthorised is penalised.[10]

The explanation of this most significant phenomenon must go beyond the analysis of a rational behaviour. It is rooted in the unconditional belief that political (Marxist) doctrine is right and must prevail at all costs and in the existing fear and suspicion towards all non-believers. That was the attitude of communist conspirators towards bourgeois societies before the revolution and it continued to be the atttitude of the communist rulers towards the society they ruled after the revolution. Soon after they came to power they lost any genuine support they ever had among the masses of the population. This lack of support was covered by a mendacious propaganda about the achievements of the system and by the suppression of all information contrary to what they wanted the population to believe. Surprisingly, this policy proved quite effective even outside the boundaries of the Soviet Union. This fact has reinforced it and in due course it became an established feature of the system. The discrepancies between official doctrine and reality were disposed of according to the famous dictum of Lenin: 'all the worse for the facts'.[11]

It is curious how this attitude persisted in all countries which were under the Soviet influence. This seems to be due to the fact that the conditions which were at the origin of this attitude in fact never ceased to exist. The Party in power has never gained popular support and continues to distrust the population over which it rules.

This fear of truth and the reluctance to impart information leads to an endemic dearth of information available to decision makers at all levels. This is the first important symptom of the deterioration of the tissue. The second is the compulsion to false reporting. As undesirable truth is suppressed anyway, and those imparting it are likely to be penalised, there is no incentive whatsoever to truthful and exact reporting. Consequently decision makers have at their disposal information which is not only patchy but often downright false. It is obvious how this must affect the quality of decision-making.

Intelligent people, and that means many decision makers, cannot be entirely ignorant of the situation, but they are incapable of doing anything about it, and are obliged to proceed with their decision making. Such conditions have led to a practice which can be called 'planning without facts'. This term refers to a situation where people who are otherwise reasonable and responsible in all consciousness make decisions which they know are based on inadequate information. They are compelled by the system to act in this way. When something goes too obviously wrong they are accused of 'voluntarism' and are sanctioned. But this does not prevent the practice continuing with disastrous consequences for the economy.

Eradication of Dissent

The second main cause of the degradation of the tissue is the eradication of dissenting views and consequently of all meaningful discussion.

The basic motive behind this attitude of the authorities is the same as in the case of the suppression of truth: the distrust of all people outside the inner centre of power. Strict conformism becomes obligatory and all dissenting views are penalised. Some subjects become virtually taboo.[12]

A centrally planned economy by its very nature has a self-correcting capacity which is much inferior to that of a market economy. This is an obvious consequence of great centralisation of decisions. But it is exactly for that reason that the centrally planned economy has a great need of constant vigilance and a competent and prompt assessment of all that happens on the economic scene. This assessment implies as a rule criticism of what happened and of what was done or not done.

The suppression of dissenting views makes the corrective machinery of the economy ineffective. It virtually annihilates it.

It can only be added that inadequate information and eradication of dissent have cumulative effects. The decision makers are supplied with insufficient and grossly distorted information and also prevented from obtaining or formulating any critical interpretation of it. This means that decisions are bound to be defective. To make matters worse the correction machinery is prevented from working. The conclusions are obvious.

Repudiation of Fairness

The third main cause of the degradation of the economic tissue is the repudiation of fairness in human relations in general and in appointments and promotion policy in particular. It is not competence and merit but party membership and the confidence of the party apparatus which opens access to positions of responsibility.

This practice is expressed in official regulations. All high positions in the country, including high managerial positions are reserved to a selected group of persons known as the 'nomenklatura'. The criteria for their selection are political. The inclusion in that group is a privilege granted practically for life. Even dismal failure in performing one's job is 'punished' (if at all) by a transfer to another job at equivalent level. This is obviously a system which effectively prevents 'new blood' from coming into managerial ranks, hampers promotion on merit, protects incompetence and invites favouritism. Managerial positions at lower levels are not reserved for the 'nomenklatura', but appointment practice is similar: the support of respective party committees is decisive. This system is certainly most effective in making sure that managerial positions are occupied by incompetent people.

After they have been appointed the managers continue to be treated unfairly. They are subject to the principle of duality of control. Apart from the usual administrative channels of control in government departments and enterprises, there are also channels through which the party controls the state administration and the economy. In matters which are supposed to be decided by managers, decisions are suppressed or modified or even imposed by the supervising party apparatus. The personnel appointments in particular are most strictly supervised by the party and the managers have least say about the selection of their own collaborators.

All this leads to a distortion of the normal relations between various levels of the administrative hierarchy. If a manager cannot follow his own judgement because of party interference, he is not always in a position to conform to directives coming from above without first referring them to party authorities at his own level. Neither can he count on the support from his superiors against the party at his level. This leads to distrust between decision makers at various levels of the system.

The crucial fact is that the managers have a limited control over their enterprises and yet the full responsibility for their performance. The party apparatus has control over all important matters but no responsibility for the consequences of decisions taken. As party officials are on the whole even less competent than managers, the results are disastrous for the economy and demoralising for the managers.

In such conditions there is a natural tendency on the part of the managers to protect themselves against being held responsible for decisions which were imposed on them against their better judgement or induced by various influences and the ever present necessity to conform to the whims of the party apparatus. When they make decisions which they think best, on the merits of the case, they become particularly vulnerable when their judgement is questioned in some influential quarters. They cannot rely on any support from their superiors.

As a safeguard against these dangers the decision makers at all levels came to rely more and more on strict procedural regulations and to insist on hard targets for the fulfilment of all tasks. It was assumed that by adhering to regulations and fulfilling the targets decision makers could achieve a degree of immunity against biased and irresponsible criticism. It is this tendency that brought about an increasing rigidity of both procedures and targets.

A tendency to cover all possible cases arising in the management of the national economy by officially issued rules has led to the proliferation of regulations and their increased complexity. Yet this complexity has not been enough to cover all cases and to replace the informed and fair judgement of the decision makers. The complexity and rigidity of the regulations has become a curse on the economy. It has prevented decision makers at all levels from exerting their judgement. It has stifled initiative and rewarded dull conformism.

The rigidity of plan targets means that it is impossible or very difficult to modify the plan in response to changing conditions. The complexity of planning procedures contributes to that difficulty. Another consequence of rigidity is the persistence of contradictions between various plan targets. Even obvious errors which are discovered after the plan has been approved are exceedingly difficult to correct.

Excessive complexity of regulations and unreasonable rigidity of targets may be considered to be two particularly malignant forms of tissue deterioration. Their direct cause is found in the fact that managers are incompetent and inhibited, but it has become established it prevents even competent managers from functioning properly.

The adverse consequences of these two forms of deterioration are too many to be discussed here in any detail.[13]

Conclusions

It may be useful to re-state briefly the main causes, symptoms and consequences of the rot which has degraded the tissue of the economic structure in centrally planned systems.

The causes were: suppression of the truth, eradication of dissent and repudiation of fairness. They all added up to what might be described as the elimination of commonsense in decision making and human relation. And commonsense is a necessary ingredient in all decision making. Without it no economy can function properly.

The symptoms of tissue degradation are: faulty information and planning without facts, distorted evaluations and destruction of corrective mechanism, the incompetence and inhibitions of decision makers and an absurd complexity of procedures and rigidity of targets.[14]

There seem to be no doubt now that tissue degradation has been a major cause of the mediocre performance of centrally planned economies.[15] It may even seem surprising that in such conditions the performance was not even worse. The failures of reforms may be attributed to the fact that degradation of the tissue was never recognised as the cause of the malaise and never adequately dealt with in any of the reforms. But this is no accident. An effective reform must reinstate the rule of commonsense and bring about conditions in which decision makers will be able to make rational and enlightened decisions. It must strike at the roots of the degradation: it must restore the appreciation of truth, recognise the value of reliable information, encourage nonconformist critical opinions, acknowledge the need for competence in all work positions and in decision making positions in particular, accept the principle of promotion on merit and of fairness between superiors and subordinates.

To achieve that, changes in the system must go both deeper and in a different direction than the reforms undertaken so far. To make it quite explicit: it is not a question of material incentives or even of changing the structure or the organisation of the national economy, or of modifying the principles of planning or introducing a degree of decentralisation. None of these merely economic reforms can be effective. What is needed is no less than a radical change in the political foundations of the system.[16]

Once the causes, symptoms and consequences of tissue deterioration have been understood, there should be no doubt that its origin can be traced to the nature of the Soviet-type system and more precisely to the suppression of human rights and political freedoms. It is ironic that the system which has first applied central economic planning at the same time created conditions which were bound to make it ineffective. The system has been born with a congenital disease which makes its economic performance incurably impaired. What is called the 'Polish Disease' is not limited to Poland. It is only that in Poland its symptoms have come dramatically into the open to be seen by all. As the causes for that condition exist in all Soviet-type economies the disease is present in all countries of the Soviet bloc, though in various degrees. It seems that the effects of the rot in the tissue have a tendency to cumulate through time and also to be more pernicious when the economy becomes more sophisticated and more technically advanced.[17] Inept management becomes then particularly harmful. This is certainly one of the main causes of the spectacular deterioration of the performance of all centrally planned economies which has been in evidence lately.

An effective remedy against the disease can only be found in the restoration of the basic human freedoms and democratic rights. But a change of that kind would be nothing else but a revolutionary transformation of the system. There is no doubt that it would encounter resistance from the Party actually in power and naturally enough would be labelled a 'counter-revolutionary' attempt. This is why the prospects for reversing the economic decline of Soviet-type economies are not bright. The deterioration of economic performance breeds discontent and has several times set in motion protest movements which would press for economic and political change. But such movements were always sooner or later suppressed by force and opportunities for an effective economic and political reform were always frustrated.

The Polish experience of August 1980 is most illuminating in this respect. It is remarkable that the striking workers have given priority to political demands. They had an intuitive perception of the essential and were not ready to limit their claims to wages and working conditions. The democratisation movement started by 'Solidarity' could have been the beginning of an effective improvement in the performance of the Polish economy as it called for reforms which in the long run could have stopped and reversed the deterioration of the economic tissue. Unfortunately, the military takeover of December 1981 put an end to the 'Solidarity' movement. It seems now unavoidable that the degradation of the tissue will continue to exert its debilitating influence on the Polish economy.

Implications of the Tissue Analysis for Economic Theory

The policy implications of the economic tissue analysis have been outlined above. However, there are also some implications of that analysis for theory, which may be worth mentioning, if only very briefly.

The problem of economic tissue has so far been placed below a threshold of interest of mainstream economics. A satisfactory state of the tissue is tacitly taken for granted and all economic analysis is based on this assumption. That practice could be questioned.

It has been shown above that the state of the tissue may vary widely. A satisfactory state of the tissue is only a special case on one end of the spectrum.

The state of the tissue could therefore be seen as a set of variables which would express inherent characteristics of the economic system.[18] Their acceptance as an element of economic analysis would mean that the usual level of abstraction on which economic analysis is conducted has been lowered by dropping the assumption about satisfactory state of the tissue. This would widen the scope of economic analysis and open possibilities for dealing with some significant problems which so far have been left beyond its scope.

The tissue analysis was applied here to centrally planned economies only. It seemed to be of crucial relevance there. However it may be suggested that the degradation of economic tissue is a problem not necessarily limited to centrally planned systems. It may well affect market and mixed systems too. It will reflect the imperfect behaviour of both managers and of the workers in fulfilling their respective obligations in the process of production. The causes of degradation as well as some of its symptoms may be different there[19] but the consequences of degradation will essentially be the same: an impairment of the performance of the economy.

It could therefore be suggested that a study of tissue problems may have a significance for a better understanding of the functioning of all economic systems and that it deserves recognition as a legitimate part of economic theory.

Notes

1. The literature of the subject is extensive. To quote just a few books on the subject. J. Wilczynski, 1972, 'Socialist Economic Development and Reforms', Macmillan, London. Alec Nove, 1981, 'The Soviet Economic System', 2nd edn, George Allen & Unwin, London. H.H. Hohmann, M. Kaser, K.C. Thalheim (eds.), 1975, 'The New Economic Systems of Eastern Europe', C. Hurst & Co., London. Ian Jeffries (ed.), 1981, 'The Industrial Enterprise in Eastern Europe', Praeger Special Studies, Holt Saunders Ltd, Eastbourne. P.J.D. Wiles, 1977, 'Economic Institutions Compared', Blackwell, Oxford. M. Bornstein, 1979, Economic Reform in Eastern Europe, 'Comparative Economic Systems', Irwin, Homewood, Ill. J.G. Zieliński, 1978, On System Remodelling in Poland, 'Soviet Studies', No. 1.

2. This is a feature of all centrally planned economies although the failures are more acute in some cases than in others. The author draws primarily from his knowledge of the Polish economy, but no doubt similar phenomena can be observed in the Soviet Union and other East European countries. Hungary and Yugoslavia must be set apart as special cases, as they have modified considerably the Soviet type system and each of them has developed its own model of a planned economy. But even there economic performance is less satisfactory than expected. It seems, therefore, that there is more than enough evidence to warrant some general conclusions about centrally planned economies which are attempted in the present paper.

3. O. Lange, 1938, 'On the Economic Theory of Socialism', Univ. of Minnesota Press, Minneapolis.

4. Lange's faults are certainly very grave, but need not be discussed here as they do not affect the argument presented below.

5. Lange, 'On the Economic Theory . . .', pp. 106 ff.

6. The memorable Baltic coast riots in Poland of December 1970 put an abrupt end to an elaborate and highly advertised system of material incentives which was the pride of planners at that time.

7. There were several reasons for that, which probably could be explained, but cannot be discussed here in any detail. They fall into two main categories: reluctance to deviate from traditional methods of economic analysis and the political sensibility of such inquiry.

8. Exceptions to this rule do of course exist. E.g. problems of information have been discussed extensively. But the obstacles to perfect information were considered to be mainly technical expressed in terms of time and costs. They have nothing to do with the condition of the tissue. Quite a different category of causes leading to imperfect information will be discussed below.

Economic consequences of corruption evidently belong to 'tissue' problems. They have been occasionally examined. They certainly deserve attention, but will not be discussed here as their significance is marginal compared with other 'tissue' problems.

9. The common element is derived mainly from the fact that the system prevailing in those countries was introduced there under the influence of the Soviet Union. It is therefore in the pecularities of the Soviet system that we must look for the origins of the phenomenon in question.

10. It is hardly believable to what lengths the suppression of information was carried. In the Stalinist period in Poland the elaboration of a number of economic indices was discontinued (including the family expenditure index) and the publication of the Statistical Yearbook was suspended.(!) Things have improved since that time, but even at present the gaps in generally available information are appalling. E.g. no reliable information on the foreign debts of Poland was apparently available even to the highest level of economic hierarchy until the situation became critical.

11. I feel sure that I have heard this saying being attributed to Lenin, but I confess I was not able to trace it to any of Lenin's writing. In my endeavours to confirm my conviction I came across a view that the saying does not belong to Lenin at all. It may be so, but 'si non e vero e ben trovato'.

12. Such as the remuneration of party officials and of the security forces. Also all problems of foreign trade especially with the Soviet Union.

13. One example is worth mentioning as it explains the failure of all attempts to improve efficiency by various incentive proposals. It was argued that no excessive hopes should be attached to such proposals. But if any possibilities existed at all in this respect, they have been consistently frustrated by the complexity and rigidity of the incentive schemes.

14. Blunders in economic policy and economic reverses may occur for various reasons even in the absence of tissue degradation. When tissue is degraded however the errors are more serious and the chances for their correction minimal.

15. It could probably be claimed that the relative performance of East European economies is in inverse relation to the degree of degradation of their respective economic tissues. This cannot be more than a qualitative judgement at present. When quantitative expressions for measuring the state of the tissue are devised it might be possible to express that relation in terms of correlation coefficients.

16. The argument that political change is an essential element of economic reform has for a long time been anathema to all 'revisionists'. Its validity has come to be widely recognised at present.

17. This was evidently the case with Poland which sank into the present acute crisis after a period of expansion, technical advance and relative prosperity enjoyed in the years 1971–5.

18. There is no doubt that when this approach is adopted some methodological problems will have to be tackled. When tissue conditions are seen as a set of variables they must eventually be given some quantitative expressions. The solution of that problem can certainly be attempted. All that is needed is ingenuity and econometric skill. The latter is available in high quality. It is, rather, rewarding fields for its application that seem to be in short supply. This is one of them.

19. See for instance: J.K. Galbraith, 1981, On Succumbing to Corporate Senility, 'International Herald Tribune', 14/15 February for example of degradation of the tissue under capitalism.

4 THE ECONOMIC ENVIRONMENT IN EASTERN EUROPE

Stephen Barker

The problems facing the East European economies are well known: declining national income growth, widespread inefficiency and waste, delays in completing investment projects, transport bottlenecks, unsatisfied consumer demand, poor worker morale and continuing trade and financing problems are just some of the more obvious ones. This paper aims to analyse the current situation to see what potential exists for the development of economic crises similar to the one Poland has been experiencing since the summer of 1980. The study breaks down into three main sections: a survey of the general features of the economic environment; an analysis of how far the symptoms of Poland's 'disease' are currently apparent; and finally a look at the measures these countries have taken to avoid the development of a similar crisis. The Soviet Union is not included in the analysis. Clearly there are many similarities between the USSR's economic difficulties and those of Poland and the rest of Eastern Europe. The inefficiency of the agricultural sector and the impact of grain imports on the hard currency trade balance for example. However, the differences, simply in terms of scale, resource endowment and trade relations, put the USSR beyond the scope of this study.

The General Environment

A look at the economic environment at the general level is useful to outline any overall similarities with, or differences from, Poland that could influence the development of similar crises. It will also reinforce the important point, which is all too commonly neglected, that Eastern Europe is not an economic monolith.

Looking at Poland's development record over the past decade (Tables 4.1, 4.2, 4.3) we see rapid growth of national income in the early to mid 1970s based on high levels of accumulation and large net inflows on the hard currency trade account. This was accompanied by a rapid build up of hard currency indebtedness and the appearance of serious bottlenecks in some sectors as growth outstripped the

87

absorptive capacity of the economy. Towards the end of the decade, however, we see the effects of the authorities' belated policy response: cutbacks in the hard currency trade deficit; a declining share of national income devoted to investment and a precipitous fall in the growth of national income. A comparison with the other countries shows some broadly similar trends, most notably in a slowdown in the growth of national income and investment, although not on the same scale. It is noticeable that Romania maintained high levels of accumulation throughout the 1970s (Table 4.2), even exceeding those in Poland. There has also been a sharp decline in national income growth from the high rates of the early to mid 1970s (Table 4.1). Furthermore Romania continued to accumulate rapidly hard currency debts, whereas the other countries have slowed the growth of their indebtedness. According to official statistics the GDR and Bulgaria have avoided a sharp decline in national income growth (Table 4.1). However, the GDR now has the problem of a relatively high debt service ratio, while Bulgaria has achieved a hard currency trade surplus and has reduced the size of her debt (Table 4.3). The Hungarian and Czechoslovakian economies have not shown particularly dynamic growth recently, but have also had some success in controlling hard currency trade and payments difficulties (Tables 4.1, 4.3).

Problems in the agricultural sector played a large part in the development of Poland's economic crisis. Looking at the structure of national income and employment in Eastern Europe (Tables 4.4 and 4.5) it is apparent that agriculture is still an important sector for these economies, although notably less so in Czechoslovakia and the GDR. Thus, as in Poland, economic performance in the area is significantly affected by fluctuations in agricultural output, whether caused by poor management or the weather. Despite the relative lesser importance of agriculture in Czechoslovakia and the GDR they are not exempt from such problems either. Bad harvests in these two countries boost the requirement for hard currency feed imports and thereby increase the constraints in the trade balance.

The orientation of foreign trade reveals some interesting differences between the East European economies. Three of these countries, Bulgaria, Czechoslovakia and the GDR, conduct two thirds or more of their trade with Communist countries (Table 4.6).

Such trade is conducted predominantly in soft currencies. Bulgaria is notable in that it conducts over half its trade with the USSR, which reflects the latter's important role as a supplier of energy and raw materials. Trade with Socialist countries is less important for Hungary,

Romania and Poland, with the proportion falling to 40 per cent in the case of Romania. On the other side of the coin these three countries are more involved in trading with the Developed West. This trade is conducted on a hard currency basis and accounts for around a third of their trade in each case, as opposed to a quarter or less for the GDR, Czechoslovakia and Bulgaria. As a final observation Romania stands out by conducting a high proportion of its foreign trade with LDC's, reflecting the impact of oil imports from the Middle East; for unlike the other countries Romania does not receive substantial supplies from the Soviet Union.

All the East European countries are prone to hard currency payments problems to some degree because, in general, their manufactured exports face stiffer competition in Western markets than within the Communist bloc. At the same time they rely on imports from the West as valuable source of high quality and technologically advanced inputs. However, because of the orientation of their trade, it is apparent that some of these countries are more prone to hard currency payments problems than others (even if their development strategy does not lead to them, as it did with Poland). Obviously this orientation of trade relations is partly dictated by the commodity structure of trade, but politics and ideology are also influential. Thus it is unlikely that the USSR would tolerate its closer political allies (Bulgaria, Czechoslovakia and the GDR) developing over-strong economic relations with the Developed West. (The GDR's special relationship with the FRG is clearly an exception, however.) In fact the Czechoslovak leadership itself seems to have ideological objections to such links, which possibly reflects a continuing hangover from 1968. On the other hand Romania has a political interest in maintaining strong economic links with the West, and is already a member of the IMF and IBRD. Hungary and Poland have also recently applied for IMF membership and Hungarian membership has been accepted.

Finally it may be worth considering the relative sizes of these economies. Several points arise from this. All these countries have important economic links with the USSR, both through trade and CMEA cooperation and specialisation. Leaving aside political considerations it is apparent that it is easier for the USSR to grant preferential terms and supplies in trade with smaller economies, such as Bulgaria, than to larger ones, such as Poland, because the size of the commitment of the Soviet Union's own resources is correspondingly smaller. This may become particularly significant with regard to energy and raw materials supplies in the 1980s. Similarly it would be easier for the USSR, and Western governments and creditors, to rescue a smaller economy from growing difficulties, for the same reasons.

How far are the Symptoms of the Polish Disease Apparent in Eastern Europe?

One of the clearest indications of the escalation of Poland's economic crisis has been the sharp downturn in national income growth (Table 4.1). In 1979 Poland recorded negative national income growth for the first time since the war, the situation worsened in 1980, and as the crisis has reached more dramatic proportions the fall in 1981 was 13 per cent. In common with the other East European countries the Polish authorities had set lower growth targets for the 1976-80 Five Year Plan (FYP), and reinforced this with the policy shift of the 'New Economic Manoeuvre' at the end of 1976. However, one striking aspect of Poland's economic record in the last FYP is the growing disparity between planned and actual performance, pointing to the authorities' increasing inability to predict and control developments (Table 4.7). Given that the East European countries are at different stages of economic development such disparities between planned and actual performances are better indicators of potential problems than absolute levels of growth. (The lesser developed economies of Bulgaria and Romania would be expected to grow more rapidly on an extensive basis than the more developed economies of Czechoslovakia and the GDR for example.) Bearing in mind that the exhortatory function of plan targets may vary between the countries, it is evident that Hungary and Romania also achieved notably poor results in 1980, both absolutely and in comparison with plan goals. The question is how far such poor performance reflects the authorities' determination to pursue adjustment policies, despite the adverse effects on overall performance, rather than a loss of control over the economy. The former would seem to be more true of Hungary than Romania.

Growing hard currency trade and payments problems were another obvious symptom of Poland's developing crisis. There are some marked variations among the other East European countries in this respect. Table 4.3 shows that Bulgaria, Hungary and Czechoslovakia have had some success in curbing adverse hard currency merchandise trade balances. Indeed, Bulgaria has managed to build up a respectable surplus. The GDR and Romania on the other hand continued to run large, and in the latter case increasing, hard currency trade deficits. It must also be remembered, however, that all these countries, with the exception of Romania, have been running trade deficits with the USSR, which the latter may seek to redress as it tackles its own economic problems in the 1980s. Similarly, these countries face varying problems in financing and controlling the growth of hard currency indebtedness. Bulgaria's convertible currency trade surpluses have enabled it to reduce the size of its debt, while Hungary and Czechoslovakia have managed to slow the growth of their indebtedness appreciably. (Furthermore Czechoslovakia has a relatively small debt in absolute terms.) The GDR and Romania are in a less favourable position, however; the former having a high debt service ratio and the latter facing especial difficulties. Payments arrears have built up, and with a large amount of short term debt and low assets Romania is currently facing a difficult liquidity crisis. In addition Romania is having debt financing problems, partly as a result of the hardening of lenders' attitudes to Eastern Europe in the wake of the Polish crisis. As a result Romania has recently been impelled to approach Western creditors to negotiate rescheduling some payments.

One of the major weaknesses of the Polish economy in the 1970s was the agricultural sector. Prime causes of this were a poor overall policy, with this sector being starved of investment and incentives, and mismanagement at the local level. In addition to this Poland was certainly not fortunate with climatic conditions; although it can be argued that problems caused by the weather could have been alleviated had agriculture received sufficient investment. The main results of poor agricultural performance were two fold: the growth of serious food shortages and a further deterioration in the trade account (due to lost food exports and an increased import requirement for grain). Similar difficulties are clearly apparent elsewhere in Eastern Europe. Romania suffers from both these problems, and for much the same reasons. Ceausescu has publicly acknowledged that agriculture has been mistakenly neglected in the drive for rapid industrial growth and has recently focused particular attention on failures within this sector The results of this are evident by the recent introduction of rationing for certain food items. Ceausescu has also stressed that poor agricultural performance is adversely affecting the trade balance. Agriculture is also causing problems for Czechoslovakia and the GDR. The leaderships of both countries recently drew attention to the difficulties caused by hard currency imports of grain for livestock feed. Indeed Honecker compared the significance of the grain problem with that of crude oil! Bulgaria and Hungary are generally self-sufficient in agriculture. Hungary's successful agricultural policy provides benefits in the form of exports of agricultural produce which are a valuable bargaining counter in intra-bloc trade.

The failure of investment policy was another major factor contributing to Poland's slide into economic catastrophe. This displayed three main failings. Firstly investment strategy failed at both macro- and micro-levels. The agricultural, transport, energy and consumer sectors were seriously neglected while those sectors that were favoured, such as engineering and metallurgy, proved to be unfortunate choices in the wake of the energy crisis and ensuing world recession. At the micro-level there are numerous instances of faulty investment decisions leading to inappropriate and delayed production. Secondly Poland invested at too high a level for too long. Lack of investment discipline meant that targets were over-shot, the absorptive capacity of the economy was exceeded, and the result was production bottlenecks and an overstraining of the transport and energy infrastructure. Finally belated investment cutbacks had to be drastic (Table 4.1) resulting in the abandonment or extensive delaying of many projects. As a result of this Poland is now seeking co-operation with other CMEA countries for the completion of such projects.

Czechoslovakia and Romania provide examples of failures in investment strategy elsewhere in Eastern Europe, albeit in different respects. The Czechoslovak authorities are particularly concerned over the growing uncompetitiveness of the traditionally successful engineering industry. This sector is now producing an excessive range of increasingly obsolescent items; the penalty of meagre attempts to introduce new technology and licences in the past. Romania on the other hand has invested heavily particularly in the petrochemicals sector and is now suffering due to adverse price movements in the oil trade. The country's own oil production has been declining resulting in an increasing import requirement. However, unlike the other East European countries Romania does not receive the larger part of its oil imports at concessionary prices from the Soviet Union. Thus the country has faced the full effect of increased world crude prices. At the same time earnings from the export of oil products have been subject to declining profitability. As a result Romania now has considerable unutilised refining capacity. This is in addition to the problems that have already been noted stemming from past neglect of agriculture's investment needs, which is now directly affecting the trade balance and the consumer.

So far, however, none of the other East European countries has been forced to implement the same type of damaging investment cutbacks that became necessary in Poland. There have been some sharp fluctuations though; for example the case of Hungary. This was partly a result of the emergence and correction of excessive levels of stockbuilding, however, allied with efforts to increase the efficiency of investment outlays in accordance with the policy of the New Economic Mechanism.

Poland's problems were eventually brought to a head by a wave of popular discontent, caused to a great extent by the government's failure to meet rising expectations over living standards (which had been fuelled by rapid increases in incomes during the boom of the early to mid seventies) and the frustration engendered by growing shortages and poor housing. Because the other East European countries are at different stages of development consumer expectations are likely to differ accordingly. Furthermore the level of expectations in the GDR, Hungary and Czechoslovakia is raised by greater exposure to the higher living standards in Western Europe. Thus a comparison of absolute living standards in Eastern Europe, apart from being inherently diffi-cult, may not be particularly helpful in judging how far Poland's economic problems may occur elsewhere. It may be more useful to examine how far the other countries are affected by the type of prob-lems that led to the powerful expression of popular dissatisfaction in Poland.

There are shortages of consumer goods of varying degrees through-out Eastern Europe, but it is generally acknowledged that Hungary has the best overall level of supplies. On the other hand the Romanian consumer is undoubtedly the worst off. Press reports of a marked deterioration in food supplies over the past eighteen months have been followed recently by the introduction of rationing and strict measures to combat hoarding. Living standards throughout the area have been coming under increasing pressure from inflation as these countries gradually abandoned strict adherence to a policy of price stability during the 1976–80 FYP. Reliable statistics are not always available on the level of consumer price inflation, and the picture is obviously clouded by problems such as 'disguised' price increases and a lack of knowledge about the large 'black' and 'grey' sectors. Nevertheless both Hungary and Czechoslovakia have publicly acknowledged that living standards are likely to stagnate in the immediate future and Romania is planning a deceleration in the growth of real incomes. Whether dis-content over living standards will lead to open protest as in Poland remains to be seen, and this is obviously dependent on many non-economic factors. However the most serious example of such protest in recent years was in Romania with a large scale strike by miners in the Jiu valley in 1977. Reports have also filtered out of the country of similar disturbances in autumn 1981.

Policy Implementation and Reform

The fact that Poland's economic crisis reached such disastrous proportions was in a large part due to the inability to implement necessary
remedial measures. The need for such action was certainly recognised;
the 'New Economic Manoeuvre' and the continuing lively debate over
reforms were a testimony to that. However, concrete policy initiatives
(such as the attempt to change the pattern of landholding via the
provision of agricultural pensions) proved to be piecemeal and ineffective. This failure to introduce effective measures to stop Poland's
economic slide was caused by several factors: inefficiency and mal-
administration; vested interests and corruption; policy constraints and
systemic weaknesses. There is plenty of anecdotal evidence of corruption and inefficiency in the other East European economies. However,
the relative levels of such activity are virtually impossible to quantify.
Similarly just as the Polish government was reticent over introducing
urgently needed retail price increases after the experiences of 1970
and 1976 there are limitations on the authorities' freedom of action in
the Policy sphere elsewhere in Eastern Europe. Thus, for example, the
Hungarian government has taken special care to prepare the population
for retail price increases and Romania has twice announced cuts in
defence expenditure supposedly to benefit the consumer.

With respect to systemic reform Poland has been something of an
exception, however (prior to the debate over economic reform assuming real content with the emergence of Solidarity). Despite the informed debate at all levels of society Poland lagged behind her neigh-
bours after the withering of the WOG (Large Economic Associations)
experiment in the mid 1970s. Elsewhere Hungary resuscitated the NEM
(New Economic Mechanism) and has pursued it with renewed commitment since 1978. The GDR has re-organised industry with the creation
of Kombinate, while Czechoslovakia followed the three year 'Ler
experiment' (1978–80) with the introduction of the 'Complex Set of
Measures' in the present FYP. Bulgaria introduced 'self accounting'
principles in agriculture in 1979 and has since extended them to industry and other sectors, and Romania has operated its own Economic
Mechanism since 1977. Questions remain as to how rigorously these
reforms are being implemented and how effective they are. Hungary has
certainly followed up the implementation of the NEM after a break in
the mid 1970s, and the relatively high living standard and recent success
in skirting hard currency trade and payments difficulties have been
quoted as evidence of its success. However, economic growth is stagnating

and the policy of shaking out surplus labour could cause socio-political problems if it is fully implemented. The efficacy of systemic changes in Bulgaria and the GDR would seem to be reflected in the continued rapid growth of output, at least according to official figures. Failures to implement planned reforms have drawn scathing official criticism in Romania and Czechoslovakia, however. The Czechoslovak authorities have blamed this on the inability and unwillingness of enterprise directors and bureaucrats, but ideological splits within the leadership may also be partly responsible. In Romania the central authorities appear to have retained tight control over economic affairs despite the avowed intention of devolving powers to enterprises and workers.

Conclusions

Looking at the economic environment in Eastern Europe some of the symptoms of Poland's economic illness are clearly present elsewhere. Romania seems to have developed many of them: a rapid deterioration in the hard currency trade and payments situation; disequilibria due to a high level of accumulation and past mistakes in investment policy; poor agricultural performance acting as a brake on economic performance, rumblings of popular discontent over poor living standards and a poor record on the implementation of reforms. The GDR has burgeoning payments difficulties and is likely to face a period of painful re-adjustment in the 1980s, especially as energy, raw materials and labour contraints begin to bite harder. All the countries are likely to have problems in ensuring adequate growth of living standards as national income growth continues to decline.

This analysis has focused on the economic environment in Eastern Europe with reference to the unfolding of Poland's economic crisis. However, it would be misleading to think that the growth of problems in the other countries will necessarily follow the same lines. There are real differences between these economies, both in their resource endowments and development strategies. Thus we may well see the appearance of, for example, the 'East German economic disease', particularly as the Polish crisis has exacerbated many of Eastern Europe's economic problems, especially those connected with energy, trade and finance. Any new crisis is likely to differ from Poland's if only because Poland has served as a warning example, not only to the other East European countries, but to the USSR and Western governments and creditors as well.

Note: Some figures in Tables 4.1–4.5 have been taken from the CMEA Statistical Yearbook as a uniform source. They may differ slightly from the figures derived from national statistics.

Figure 4.1: Eastern Europe: Selected Economic Indicators (annual percentage change)

	1971	1972	1973	1974	1975	1976	1977	1978	1979	1980
National income (net material product)										
Bulgaria	7.1	7.6	8.3	7.3	8.9	6.5	6.4	5.5	6.6	5.6
CSSR	4.5	5.6	4.7	6.2	6.3	4.0	4.3	4.1	3.1	3.0
GDR	4.6	5.6	5.9	6.1	4.7	3.5	5.3	3.7	3.6	4.3
Hungary	6.5	5.0	7.4	6.9	5.0	3.0	8.3	4.2	2.6	-0.7
Poland	8.3	10.3	11.2	10.5	9.5	7.0	4.9	3.1	-2.4	-5.2
Romania	13.9	9.8	10.8	12.6	9.8	9.9	8.7	7.6	6.1	3.0
Global industrial production										
Bulgaria	8.9	9.1	9.2	8.2	8.5	6.7	6.9	6.8	5.5	4.2
CSSR	6.7	6.8	6.4	6.5	6.9	5.7	5.4	5.1	3.8	3.3
GDR	5.5	6.3	6.9	7.4	6.4	6.0	4.6	4.7	4.5	4.7
Hungary	6.7	4.8	7.4	8.2	4.8	4.6	6.5	4.8	3.2	-1.6
Poland	8.1	10.4	11.3	11.5	11.2	9.3	7.0	4.9	2.7	0.0
Romania	11.7	11.8	14.6	14.6	12.0	11.6	12.7	8.9	8.2	6.5
Global agricultural production										
Bulgaria	1.4	5.7	1.3	-1.3	7.4	4.4	-4.8	4.4	6.0	-5.1
CSSR	3.3	3.9	4.5	2.2	-1.4	-2.2	9.6	2.0	-3.9	6.2
GDR	0.0	10.7	-0.8	7.3	-3.0	-4.6	6.5	2.8	2.2	0.0
Hungary	9.0	3.0	6.6	3.4	1.3	-2.6	10.7	1.8	-1.2	3.6
Poland	3.2	8.5	7.8	1.3	-1.9	-1.4	1.4	2.7	-1.3	-10.7
Romania	19.4	9.5	0.6	1.2	3.0	17.1	-0.5	2.5	5.4	-4.2
Total volume of gross fixed investment										
Bulgaria	1.9	9.7	7.1	7.6	7.4	0.5	14.3	0.7	-2.2	7.6
CSSR	5.1	8.5	9.5	9.2	8.4	3.9	2.9	4.0	1.6	1.5
GDR	0.5	3.9	8.0	4.3	3.8	7.3	5.4	3.1	2.0	0.6
Hungary	11.3	-1.2	3.7	9.1	13.5	0.0	12.8	5.0	1.1	-6.0
Poland	7.3	23.6	25.0	22.4	14.4	2.1	4.3	1.6	-7.0	-10.0
Romania	10.7	10.3	8.1	13.3	15.2	8.4	11.6	16.0	4.1	3.0

Sources: Calculated from CMEA Statistical Yearbook 1976, 1981

Table 4.2: Eastern Europe: Utilisation of National Income (percentage shares)

	1970	1971	1972	1973	1974	1975	1976	1977	1978	1979	1980
Accumulation fund											
Bulgaria	29.2	23.6	26.7	27.7	30.8	32.5	28.6	26.0	24.0	22.8	22.4
CSSR	27.0	25.7	26.0	26.9	28.6	29.2	28.7	25.1	24.9	24.9	25.2
GDR	24.3	22.8	22.1	22.7	22.6	22.3	23.0	23.3	21.6	20.5	22.6
Hungary	24.9	30.4	26.4	25.5	29.6	27.7	27.2	28.2	31.9	25.7	23.0
Poland			1971/5: 34.1					1976/80: 36.3			
Romania	25.1	29.3	31.7	34.6	37.2	34.1	34.7	31.7	30.8	25.1	17.9
Consumption fund											
Bulgaria	70.8	76.4	73.3	72.3	69.2	67.5	71.4	74.0	76.0	77.2	77.6
CSSR	73.0	74.3	74.0	73.1	71.4	70.8	71.3	74.9	75.1	75.1	74.8
GDR	75.7	77.2	77.9	77.3	77.4	77.7	77.0	76.7	78.4	79.5	77.4
Hungary	75.1	69.6	73.6	74.5	70.4	72.3	72.8	71.8	68.1	74.3	77.0
Poland			1971/5: 65.9					1976/80: 63.7			
Romania	74.9	70.7	68.3	65.4	62.8	65.9	65.3	68.3	69.2	74.9	82.1

Sources: CMEA Statistical Yearbook 1973, 1974, 1976, 1981.

Table 4.3: Eastern Europe: Hard Currency Trade and Payments

	1975	1976	1977	1978	1979	1980
	Visible Trade Balance with Community Countries (Million US $)					
Bulgaria	−561	−228	+ 8	+ 184	+ 768	+ 946
CSSR	−366	−599	−625	−427	−484	+ 7
GDR	−1078	−1534	−1477	−1094	−2020	−1719
Hungary	−773	−605	−875	−1347	−682	−677
Poland	−2673	−2932	−2156	−1890	−2007	−818
Romania	−132	−3	−48	−944	−1320	−1462
	Gross Hard Currency Debt (Billion US $ end of year)					
Bulgaria	2.6	3.2	3.7	4.2	4.5	4.0[c]
CSSR	1.1	1.9	2.6	3.2	4.0	4.5[c]
GDR	5.2	5.9	7.1	8.9	10.1	12.5[c]
Hungary	3.1	4.0	5.7	7.5	8.0	8.2[c]
Poland	7.6	11.2	14.3	16.9	20.5	23.0
Romania	2.9	2.9	3.6	5.2	7.0	
	Debt Service Ratio[a]					
Bulgaria	33	39	45	47	36	30[c]
CSSR	14	15	17	20	22	25[c]
GDR	25	29	37	46	55	55[c]
Hungary	19	21	25	36	36	35[c]
Poland[b]	26	34	46	61	75	82
Romania	23	18	19	21	24	30[c]

Notes: a. Repayments on medium and long term debt as a share of merchandise exports to non Communist countries.
b. Percentage ratio between debt service and exports of goods and services.
c. Estimates.

Sources: Trade data; East European Official Statistics. Debt figures, see J.P. Zoeter, p. 716, East European Economic Assessment, A Compendium of Papers submitted to the Joint Economic Committee, Congress of the United States, July 1981. Data on Poland's debt position are taken from the Government Report on the State of the Economy, July 1981.

Table 4.4: Eastern Europe: Structure of Produced National Income by Branches of the Economy (percentage shares)

	1960	1970	1975	1976	1977	1978	1979	1980
				Industry				
Bulgaria	47.3	51.1	52.1	52.0	52.8	56.5	56.6	51.8
CSSR	63.4	62.1	65.7	68.2	61.1	61.1	64.8	64.8
GDR	62.6	57.8	59.1	60.3	61.9	64.8	68.7	68.3
Hungary	37.6	44.1	46.2	47.2	46.3	46.7	48.6	49.5
Poland	46.9	54.6	59.6	51.8	52.5	52.2	52.9	54.7
Romania	42.1	59.1	57.1	56.6	57.8	58.7	59.5	59.3
				Agriculture and Forestry				
Bulgaria	32.3	22.8	22.1	21.4	18.4	18.4	19.5	16.7
CSSR	15.2	10.5	8.7	7.7	9.1	8.5	6.6	7.3
GDR	12.2	12.8	11.1	9.8	10.2	9.0	9.2	8.5
Hungary[a]	29.8	21.7	17.9	16.1	17.3	16.2	15.2	15.8
Poland	25.8	17.3	14.8	15.5	15.6	16.0	15.7	15.3
Romania	34.9	19.5	16.6	19.0	16.7	15.9	15.5	15.2
				Other[b]				
Bulgaria	20.4	26.1	25.8	26.6	28.8	25.1	23.9	31.5
CSSR	21.4	27.4	25.6	24.1	29.8	30.4	28.6	27.9
GDR	25.2	29.4	29.8	29.9	27.9	26.2	22.1	23.2
Hungary	32.6	34.2	35.9	36.7	36.4	37.1	36.2	34.7
Poland	27.3	28.1	25.6	32.7	31.9	31.8	31.4	30.0
Romania	23.0	21.4	26.3	24.4	25.5	25.4	25.0	25.5

Notes: a. Agriculture only.
   b. Construction, Transport and Communications, Trade, Material and Technical Supplies, Services and Procurements and other
      sectors of material production.
Source: CMEA Statistical Yearbook 1981.

Table 4.5: Eastern Europe: Structure of Employment (percent)

	1960	1970	1975	1976	1977	1978	1979	1980
				Industry and Construction				
Bulgaria	27.1	38.8	41.5	41.9	42.5	42.9	43.2	43.2
CSSR	46.0	47.3	48.3	48.2	48.1	48.1	48.0	47.8
GDR	48.3	49.6	50.9	51.0	51.2	51.1	51.1	50.9
Hungary	34.0	43.2	43.8	43.3	42.9	42.8	42.3	41.1
Poland	32.4	37.6	39.8	39.6	40.8	40.8	40.9	40.8
Romania	20.0	30.8	38.7	40.2	41.4	42.4	43.8	43.8
				Agriculture and Forestry				
Bulgaria	55.5	35.8	28.2	26.8	25.9	25.2	24.9	24.5
CSSR	26.0	18.5	15.7	15.3	14.9	14.5	14.3	14.2
GDR	17.2	13.0	11.1	10.8	10.7	10.6	10.5	10.5
Hungary	38.9	26.4	22.6	22.2	21.9	21.7	21.8	22.0
Poland	44.1	34.6	30.8	30.7	28.2	27.6	26.9	26.3
Romania	65.6	49.3	38.1	35.9	34.7	32.8	31.0	29.8
				Other[a]				
Bulgaria	17.4	25.4	30.3	31.3	31.6	31.9	31.9	32.3
CSSR	28.0	34.2	36.0	36.5	37.0	37.4	37.7	38.0
GDR	34.5	37.4	38.0	38.2	38.1	38.3	38.4	38.6
Hungary	27.1	30.4	33.6	34.5	35.2	35.5	35.9	36.6
Poland	23.5	27.8	29.4	29.7	31.0	31.6	32.2	32.9
Romania	14.4	19.9	23.2	23.9	23.9	24.8	25.2	26.4

Note: a. Transport and Communications, Trade, Material and Technical Supplies Service and Procurements and the non-productive sector.
Source: CMEA Statistical Yearbook 1981.

Table 4.6: Eastern Europe: Orientation of Visible Foreign Trade (percentage shares)

	Trade Turnover	Imports	Exports		Trade Turnover	Imports	Exports
Bulgaria (1980)				**Hungary (1980)**			
Socialist countries	74.8	78.8	71.1	Socialist countries	52.7	50.6	55.1
of which USSR	53.5	57.2	50.1	of which USSR	28.4	27.7	29.3
Developed West	16.5	17.2	15.9	Developed West	34.3	38.3	30.1
LDCs	8.6	4.0	13.0	LDCs	12.9	11.1	14.8
CSSR (1980)				**Poland (1980)**			
Socialist countries	69.8	70.2	69.6	Socialist countries	55.6	55.5	55.8
of which USSR	35.8	36.0	35.7	of which USSR	32.2	33.2	31.2
Developed West	23.0	24.4	21.8	Developed West	32.7	32.0	33.6
LDCs	7.0	5.5	8.6	LDCs	11.5	12.5	10.5
GDR (1980)				**Romania (1980)**			
Socialist countries	65.9	63.3	68.7	Socialist countries	41.1	38.2	44.3
of which USSR	35.8	36.1	35.4	of which USSR	17.3	15.8	19.0
Developed West	27.4	30.5	24.1	Developed West	33.2	31.2	35.5
LDCs	6.7	6.2	7.2	LDCs	25.6	30.5	20.2

Source: East European Official Statistics.

Table 4.7: Eastern Europe: Planned and Actual National Income Growth

		Plan	Result			Plan	Result
Bulgaria	1976	9.0	6.5	Hungary	1976	5.0	3.0
	1977	8.2	6.3		1977	6.0	8.0
	1978	6.8	5.6		1978	5.0	4/4.5
	1979	7.0	6.6		1979	3/4	1.8
	1980	5.7	5.7		1980	3/3.5	–0.8
	1981	5.1	–		1981	2/2.5	1.8
CSSR	1976	5.0	4.0	Poland	1976	8.3	6.8
	1977	5.2	4.2		1977	5.7	5.0
	1978	4.9	4.1		1978	5.4	3.0
	1979	4.3	3.1		1979	2.8	–2.3
	1980	3.7	3.0		1980	1.4/1.8	–4.0
	1981	2.8	–		1981	–	–13.0
GDR	1976	5.3	3.6	Romania	1976	10.5	10.5
	1977	5.5	5.2		1977	11.5	8.6
	1978	5.2	3.6		1978	11/11.5	7.6
	1979	4.3	3.8		1979	8.8	6.2
	1980	4.8	4.2		1980	8.8	2.5
	1981	5.0	5.5		1981	7.0	4.2

Source: East European Official Statistics.

5 IS THERE A ROMANIAN ECONOMIC CRISIS? THE PROBLEMS OF ENERGY AND INDEBTEDNESS

Alan Smith

Introduction

The Romanian economy was faced with a number of severe economic problems in attempting to fulfil the Sixth Five-Year Plan (1976–1980), the worst of which was the rising level of hard-currency indebtedness, primarily associated with imports of crude oil and raw materials which required Romania to reschedule its short-term debt in early 1982. The principal causes of the economic difficulties were a series of natural disasters (including the March 1977 earthquake, floods and poor climatic conditions resulting in poor harvests), and a number of chance external factors which affected the supply and cost of crude oil imports (including the fall of the Shah of Iran and the doubling of world oil prices in 1979). But these in turn were severely aggravated by existing problems of domestic economic management (including over-taut planning, over-optimistic investment plans and excessive consumption of raw materials per unit of output) and by Romania's independent foreign policy which effectively isolated her from CMEA energy supplies. The principal indicators of Romania's economic difficulties can be listed as follows:

1. Declining Growth Rates

A slow down in the rate of growth of the major economic aggregates including gross and net material product, industrial output, investment, industrial labour productivity, real income, real wages etc., is apparent from Romanian data. (See Appendix A.) This is partly mitigated by the fact that the rate of growth of industrial output in 1980 (6.5 per cent) was still the highest in Eastern Europe and that the recorded growth rates of this and other aggregates were respectable in comparison with those recorded by the UK or Poland. However, the low level of Romanian living standards would mean that the failure of growth rates to rise above 1980 levels could lead to severe problems.

2. External Imbalance

Romanian data indicate that, after a period of balance in visible trade from 1975-7, trade imbalances opened up in 1978. Consequently, the accumulated deficits in trade with non-socialist countries which had remained approximately constant from 1975-7 nearly trebled by the end of 1980 (see Table 5.1). This is confirmed by Western estimates of Romania's hard currency indebtedness which indicate that this trebled from approximately 3 billion dollars at the end of 1977 to 9 billion dollars by the end of 1980.

It can be seen from Table 5.2 that the major cause of imbalance has been increased deficit on trade in fuel and raw materials which has in turn been caused by imports of crude oil not being offset by a corresponding increase in exports of refined oil products and chemicals.

3. A Progressive Decline in the Degree of Fulfilment of Industrial Output Targets

An analysis of the degree of fulfilment of the major indicators of the five-year plan is complicated by the fact that the former are established in 'comparable prices' whereas fulfilment is largely recorded in actual prices. However, where physical output targets have been established for industrial products for each year of the five-year plan these show a substantial and progressive degree of underfulfilment in each year of the plan. This phenomenon can still be observed if the oil and petrochemical industries are excluded from the calculations. As the revised annual plan targets were similarly underfulfilled, this cannot be attributed to a rational, planned response to adverse external and internal factors. The degree of underfulfilment is most severe in the energy (coal, electricity, crude oil) and iron and metal-fabricating industries (especially shipbuilding) and petrochemicals. There were, however, some substantial growth rates and in most cases the 1980 actual levels were higher than the 1976 plan targets, with the exception of industrial meat production, crude oil and television sets, while the 1980 outputs of radio sets and refrigerators were barely above 1976 plan targets.

4. Increased Savings Deposits

Romanian monetary and income data do not provide sufficient information for the calculation of an accurate balance of money incomes and expenditure. There are however some indications that planned domestic demand is running ahead of the domestic supply of goods and services and that this has 'leaked' through to foreign trade. Romanian data presented to the IMF indicate that citizens' deposits at the Savings and Loan Bank increased 2.2 times over the five year plan period,[1] rising from approximately 3-4 months' sales in state retail stores to 6 months' in 1980. (These figures exclude other money holdings on the demand side and payments for rent, housing etc. on the supply side.)

Furthermore, while the plan law for wages was overfulfilled the plan for retail sales fell midway between the targets established in the plan law while services were substantially below plan. It is however the detailed composition of fulfilment of the aggregate retail plan that gives most cause for concern. The 1980 targeted sales for butter, eggs, vegetables, fruit, footwear, radios, televisions, and refrigerators were all substantially underfulfilled. The aggregated money targets for the retail plan were only fulfilled by the sale of 15,000 cars above plan, while production of cars was actually 23,000 below plan.[2]

The most probable interpretation of these figures is that (high-priced) car sales were increased both to mop up excess demand and to provide an incentive for continued savings for those with high money balances. The failure to meet domestic production targets indicates that the impact of this was borne by the foreign trade sector. Moreover, they must have been imported, contrary to plan.

The plan communiqué for 1976–80 refers specifically to 'giving up exports of quantities of foodstuffs . . . to ensure consumption'.[3] This follows a decline in the trade surplus on foodstuffs already apparent in 1978 and 1979. Finally food price increases averaging about 35 per cent were announced in February 1982.

5. Labour Problems

There have been several reports in the West of labour disturbances and strikes. The most important of these concern the Jiu Valley, the country's principal mining region. In 1977 a miners' strike involving between 45,000 and 90,000 workers was reported. Although a change in the pension laws was cited as the immediate cause, other alleged grievances included work conditions, unpaid overtime (including voluntary Sunday work to help the economy overcome the problems caused by the March earthquake) and complaints about poor housing and infrastructure. It was further reported that Government Ministers were held hostage until Ceausescu addressed the miners in person and that the strike leaders were subsequently deported from the area. Later in 1979 attempts to establish free trade unions in the area were also reported, while on this occasion grievances were said to include human rights issues (particularly involving the Hungarian and German minorities) as well as economic matters.[4] Finally, there have been reports of a hostile reception for Ceausescu in the area in autumn 1981.

Although these cannot be confirmed from Romanian publications the Communiqué on Plan Fulfilment for 1979 referred to the failure to meet plan targets 'because of an unjustified discontinued operation of installations . . . and shortcomings in labour organisation',[5] while similar references were made by Ceausescu when reviewing the fulfilment of the five-year plan.

An economic reform known as the 'New Economic-Financial Mechanism' which theoretically introduces the principle of workers' self-management was announced in March 1978. The major intentions of the reform were to increase the role of financial over physical indicators, to replace global output by net output as the major enterprise success indicator, to require enterprises to cover costs from revenues and to pay money bonuses and social-cultural expenditure out of profits. Enterprises were still to receive detailed targets for inputs, outputs, investment etc., and workers' representatives on factory committees were outnumbered by ex-officio state and party appointees.

The intention appears therefore to be to introduce greater financial probity and to give enterprises and workers a direct incentive to economise on raw materials, rather than to introduce marketisation, while the enhanced role of workers' committees appears to be primarily to act as a transmission belt for centrally determined decisions.[6]

It was apparent from Ceausescu's speeches in 1980 that little progress had been made in implementing the reform and that many enterprises were still receiving budget subsidies to cover losses. The progress of the reform to date would appear to indicate that it has been initiated as a response to problems rather than being the cause of those problems, although of course the uncertainty engendered by reform proposals could have affected economic performance.

A more significant change could be the establishment of a direct link between domestic and foreign prices. The transferable rouble has been equated with the dollar and translated into a single rate for the domestic leu for the purpose of enterprise accounting, while foreign trade data from 1980 have been adjusted accordingly, leading to some initial problems of interpretation. The economic reason for the change is to enable the identification of loss-making activities particularly where these may involve importing machinery and raw materials from hard currency sources at world market prices and exporting the outputs to CMEA countries at prices based on the (lower) sliding world-market average.

The real test of the reform will be whether the Romanian authorities will be willing to close loss making plants and incur worker hostility. Ceausescu has said that where 'objective conditions' lead to losses, plants will be closed and 'workers transferred to other jobs.'[7]

Historical Background to the Crisis

Romanian economic development since 1950 has been broadly based on the classic model of 'extensive growth'. A large and expanding proportion of national income has been channelled into investment, half of which has been directed to industry while 80–90 per cent of industrial investment has been directed towards producers' goods. Consequently the proportion of National Income utilised increased from 17.6 per cent in the first five-year plan to 34.1 per cent in the fifth plan (1971–5) while the proportion of National Income invested in industrial producer goods alone increased from 8.2 per cent to 14.4 per cent over the corresponding period.[8] As a result productive industry has grown faster than the extractive industry and trade surpluses obtained on fuels and raw materials before 1960 have been transformed into growing deficits.

Industrial employment has increased from 0.8 million in 1950 to 3.2 million in 1979 with a slightly larger decline in agricultural labour (2.7 million). Although this has been partially offset by industrial deliveries to agriculture (principally machinery and fertilisers) it has placed some strain on agricultural output as the more productive labour has left the countryside. Although the balance of trade in items of agricultural origin and foodstuffs is complicated by the vagaries of the weather, no clear improvement can be discerned in these items since 1967 and the 1979 overall balance is hardly better in money terms than that obtained in 1960 (see Table 5.2). The success of the industrial strategy does however appear to be confirmed by an annual average growth rate of industrial output of 12.9 per cent between 1950 and 1977.

In 1967, while the principles of domestic economic reform were still being discussed, Romania embarked on the strategy of 'import-led growth' which was subsequently adopted in a more all-embracing form by Gierek in Poland.

The Romanian strategy was directed at raising domestic productivity through the acquisition of western technology principally via co-operation ventures with western multinationals including those involving western investment in Romania with repayment in products from the plant and finally those involving western (minority) equity participation. It appears from both western and Romanian sources that co-operation ventures were less successful than the Romanians had anticipated and the bulk of technical transfer fell on direct purchases of machinery and equipment.

Although this involved substantial short-run indebtedness Romania did not rely extensively on private bank loans in this period but looked to suppliers' credits, and official government credit support. Romania joined the IMF and the World Bank and immediately took up borrowings from those sources.[9] Simultaneously it cultivated markets in Third World countries which partly offset deficits in trade with industrial economies (Table 5.1). Data presented by Romanian authorities to the World Bank indicate that a considerable proportion of exports to Third World countries were paid for in convertible currencies while bilateral deals further enabled Romania to obtain fuel and raw materials without expending hard currency.[10] Where this involved imports of crude oil, sales of refined products to the West made this a sensible and attractive proposition.

Sales to the West did not materialise in the desired quanitites however and the resulting indebtedness caused some concern notably in France and West Germany. Although part of the reason for the failure of sales can be attributed to the classic micro-economic reasons normally associated with East European difficulties of marketing in the West — poor quality products, insufficient knowledge of market conditions, western discrimination etc. — the fact that Romania managed to increase substantially her exports of industrial consumer goods (mainly furniture, footwear and clothing) when required after 1973 indicate that macroeconomic pressures may have been present also in the period from 1967–72.

It is however noticeable that Romania, unlike Poland, did not allow excess demand to lead to imports of consumer items and substantial trade surpluses were made on foodstuffs and industrial consumer goods. Despite the shock of increased oil prices in 1974 Romania appeared to be reasonably successful in reducing its deficit in trade with non-Communist countries in the mid 1970s.

Differences between the impact of the oil price rises of 1974 and 1979 on Romania as opposed to Eastern Europe may need some explanation. The countries of Eastern Europe, with the exception of Romania, were net oil and gas importers in 1974, although they obtained most of their supplies from the USSR.

The effect of the oil crisis was therefore to worsen those countries' terms of trade with the USSR to the extent that the oil price rise was fed into the CMEA price-system by the 'Bucharest formula' which based intra-CMEA prices on a sliding average of the preceding five-years' world market prices. This formula still represented a considerable Soviet subsidy compared with existing world market prices, and the impact was further diminished by the fact that the USSR did not demand immediate full payment. In the longer run, the East European countries appear to have made about half of the resource transfers associated with the increases of the subsidised price, which still represents a reduced availability of resources to their domestic economies. As Romania was a net oil exporter in value terms until 1977 when domestic oil demand outstripped supply, she substantially avoided the initial impact of the crisis.

Two separate effects of the oil price rise can be noted in the case of the centrally-planned economies. Firstly, from the macroeconomic point of view the net oil importers are faced with reduced domestic resource availability which requires a reduction in plan targets, unless hidden reserves can be discovered. From a microeconomic point of view, the domestic plans of all economies, be they exporters or importers, require adjustment in the face of changed relative prices for imports and exports.

The macroeconomic problem involves either cutting personal consumption, through a combination of price rises, reductions in disposable income and increases in voluntary savings, or cuts in central expenditure involving investment, defence, social expenditure etc.

The separation of internal from external prices may make the microeconomic problem harder to resolve, leading to difficulties at the central level in identifying which industries to contract and which to expand and giving little incentive to enterprises to cut back their demand for relatively expensive raw materials. To the extent that this may, at best, result in a lagged response to changed world prices the macroeconomic problem will be exacerbated.

If the required cutbacks are not made overtaut planning places a burden on foreign trade planners. For either they will be required to restrict imports to preserve balance of payments equilibrium, and so create domestic bottlenecks and shortages, or a continued balance of payments deficit will be incurred which may continue until there is a foreign exchange crisis. To the extent that 'uneconomic' investment plans may continue to be pursued during this period, the later the exchange crisis is delayed the more severe the required adjustment process will be.

For largely political and institutional reasons the East European centrally planned economies pursued taut planning policies in the immediate aftermath of the oil price rises thereby creating excess demand which was felt in the investment sector. The West European economies eventually pursued deflationary policies, the multiplier effects of which created excess supply in industries not immediately affected and which were most severe in the capital goods industries. Consequently a short-run complementarity arose between Eastern and Western Europe whose exploitation was facilitated by the recycling of unspent petrocurrency earnings in European financial markets. The impact of this on the Romanian economy differed somewhat from its impact elsewhere in Eastern Europe. As a net oil exporter Romania did not suffer from the immediate macroeconomic problems resulting from the price rise, and consequently tended to isolate herself from the general problems of relative price changes. In the sixth five-year plan Romania still concentrated investment in energy-intensive industries, the result of which was to increase domestic demand for oil at the time domestic supply was falling, so that finally Romania became a net oil importer. Simultaneously Romania responded to natural disasters and diminished domestic resource availability not by cutting back plans but by pursuing taut planning policies, as a result of which macroeconomic problems started to bite.

At this stage the effect of Romania's unwillingness to enter CMEA specialisation agreements in order to pursue an 'all-round' industrialisation became crucial. In the early 1960s Romania embarked on the construction of a steel mill at Galati[11] using western assistance after it had become apparent that Khrushchev was opposed to its construction, because Romania lacked appropriate raw materials. By 1980 imported iron ore reached 16 million tons of which less than half came from the USSR, while metallurgical coke and coking coal also had to be imported, two-thirds coming from non-Communist sources, including the USA.[12]

A similar but further-reaching process has taken place with Romania's development of a diversified petrochemical industry in the 1970s, in opposition to the basic CMEA policy that petrochemical development should be predominantly sited near Soviet sources of oil and gas feedstocks. As Romania obtains only 2 per cent of its total energy supplies from CMEA this has required additional imports of crude oil from hard currency sources the cost of which doubled in 1979. Consequently crude oil imports in 1979 and 1980 reached 9.2 and 17.1 billion lei respectively and accounted for all of the deficit in trade on fuel and raw materials (see Table 5.2). Similarly the trade surplus with third-world countries has been turned into a substantial deficit (Table 5.1). Although the value of refined oil exports has increased, internal problems have resulted in oil products being diverted to domestic electricity generation (see section C). Similarly, western demand for petrochemical products and steel has declined, creating further balance of payments pressures.

As a result, the complementarity of interests between Eastern and Western Europe has been replaced in the case of Romania by competitiveness. Romania now requires imported crude oil and raw materials from hard currency sources for day to day operations, while attempting to sell products in highly competitive western markets. The problems faced by Romania are, therefore, far more severe than those faced by other East European countries (except Poland) and could be reasonably described by the word 'crisis'. A more detailed analysis of the problems is given in the next section.

The Sixth Five-year Plan (1976–80)

1. *Plan Formulation*

Since Ceausescu's accession to power in 1965 Romania's five-year plans have demonstrated a strong hortatory element with frequent upward revisions during the process of formulation and implementation. If a pattern can be discerned it is that initial Plan Directives are first approved at the Party Congress which takes place towards the end of the fourth year of the preceding plan period. The plan laws for both the fifth and sixth five-year plans were revised substantially upwards before final approval in 1971 and 1976 (see Appendix B). Finally, after the first two years of the plan in both 1972 and 1977, the plans were again revised upwards. The 1977 increase was announced in October despite the disturbances in the Jiu Valley and the March earthquake which was officially stated to have caused damage amounting to 2 billion dollars (1 billion of which was to housing) as well as causing 1,570 deaths and 9,300 serious injuries.[13] Increases in the money value of industrial output and investment were announced which were to be achieved by increased labour productivity and reduced expenditure on raw materials, while increases in wages and social security benefits were also announced. The extent to which these revisions reflected real increases over the plan law is hard to estimate as the price basis for calculating investment targets was changed for the first time since 1963 (partly reflecting increased oil prices) and subsequent actual plan fulfilments were measured in current not comparable prices. Although the public rhetoric clearly implied that these were real increases, it is interesting that the majority of physical industrial output targets specified in the 1978 annual plan that can be compared with any accuracy with annual targets established in the five year plan, were either below or in the lower range of the five-year plan targets, while only tractor output was raised above the upper-bounds of the five-year plan target.

2. *Energy and Strategy of the Sixth Five-year Plan*[14]

The sixth five-year plan continued and strengthened Romania's traditional policy of extensive growth; increasing the planned level of investment to 183 per cent of the level of the fifth five-year plan (1,000 billion lei in 1963 prices). Industry was to receive 581 billion lei (exactly equivalent to aggregate industrial investment in the period 1956-75) of which 120 billion were destined for the petrochemical industry, and 120 billion to machine tools, while steel output was planned to double. Global industrial production was planned to grow 62-70 per cent over the entire period while the output of electricity was planned to increase by 40-7 per cent. This would clearly place some strain on primary energy sources but the output of crude oil was planned to rise gradually from the 1975 level of 14.6 million tons to 15.5 millions by 1980 while the production of methane gas was planned to stabilise at 26.8 billion cubic metres (slightly below the 1975 level of 27 billion (see Table 5.4). The proportion of electric power generated by oil and gas was planned to fall from 53.8 per cent in 1975 to 33 per cent by 1980 (i.e. from 28.7 billion kwh to 25 billion kwh), reducing consumption of oil and gas by approximately 1.25 million tons of oil equivalent.

The majority of the increase in electric power generation (see Table 5.5) was to come from coalfired sources which were to rise from 27.8 per cent in 1975 to 44 per cent in 1980 (or from 14.8 billion kwh to 33 billion kwh). It is at this stage that Romanian energy plans appeared to be highly optimistic. Coal production was planned to double in weight from 27.1 million tons in 1975 to 53-56.6 million tons in 1980. Romanian 'hard coal' (whose output was planned to grow from 7.3 million tons to 9.4 million tons) has a calorific value only about half that of imported coal.[15] The majority of the increase (from 19.7 million to 47.1 million tons) was to come from low quality lignite which is uneconomic to transport over long distances. Principal deposits are to be found in Oltenia in the Jiu Valley, part of which is mined underground and part of which is opencast. Normally the calorific value of lignite at 1600–2000 kilocalories per kilogram is about 20–25 per cent of that of hard coal. Romanian lignite is reported by the World Bank to have a calorific value of between 1600 and 1970 kilocalories per kilogram.[16] At those levels the planned increase in lignite production would have substituted for 4 to 5 million tons of oil equivalent in 1980.

3. The Fulfilment of the Five-year Plan[17]

Major plan targets were fulfilled in 1976 and despite the problems referred to above, aggregated industrial targets were realised in 1977. The successful fulfilment of aggregated targets, however, concealed considerable problems in specific industrial sectors, particularly energy, that grew in importance as the plan progressed. Electricity generation in 1977 was 5 per cent below plan, primarily as a result of a 20 per cent shortfall in coal production (see Tables 5.4 and 5.5). Although methane gas production was above the target established in the five year plan actual output was a billion cubic metres below the 1976 level. As a result the amount of electricity generated by oil increased from 2.5 billion kilowatt hours to 6.3 billion, requiring an additional consumption of fuel oil of around three-quarters of a million tons. Exports of fuel oil (and exports of refined products in total) fell by 1.1 million tons, the effect being that Romania became a net importer of oil and oil products in value terms for the first time (see Table 5.4).

The emerging energy problem was further compounded by overtaut planning in 1978 much of whose impact was borne by foreign trade. Industrial investment (although below plan) grew by 20 per cent while the trade deficit in machinery and equipment which had doubled to 3.5 billion foreign exchange lei in 1977 grew to 4.9 billion in 1978 (see Table 5.2). Simultaneously the volume of domestic investment attributed to imported machinery and equipment was rapidly outgrowing the volume attributed to domestic machinery. More seriously oil output fell by a further 0.9 million tons and although coal output, lignite output and coal imports were all stated to have increased, the volume of electricity generated by coal and lignite declined and a further 0.9 million tons of oil products were diverted to electricity generation. Oil imports rose by 4.1 million tons to 12.9 million tons, and although exports of refined products increased the deficit on oil account grew to a third of a billion dollars. In 1979, the year world oil prices doubled, oil production declined by a further 1.4 million tons and natural gas by 1.8 billion cubic metres. The major impact was borne in the domestic economy with electricity output 10 per cent below plan and feedstocks to the petrochemical industry substantially reduced, enabling the volume of exports of oil products to be maintained.

In 1980 the full impact of increased energy prices, overoptimistic energy planning and taut investment plans was felt in both the domestic and external sectors of the economy. Oil output fell to 11.5 million tons — 4 million tons below the five-year plan target set in 1975 — lignite production at 27.1 million tons was no less than 20 million tons below plan, and hard coal output at 8.1 million tons was 1.3 million tons below plan. To meet the planned output of electricity of 75.0 — 78.8 billion kilowatt hours would have required the equivalent of 4.5 million tons of oil to be diverted to this sector. In fact, the equivalent of only 2.5 million tons were diverted to generating electric power which was 10 — 15 per cent below plan targets. Oil imports rose to 16 million tons at a cost of 3.82 billion dollars and the deficit on the oil account increased to 1.61 billion dollars. Consequently, although refining capacity had been increased to 33 million tons per annum during the five year plan, throughput of only 27 million tons could be maintained.

The impact of reduced throughput was most severe in the petrochemical industry, which was planned to grow by 15.2 — 16.5 per cent per annum throughout the plan but actually grew at an annual rate of 9.6 per cent (see Table 5.6). The latter figure resulted from a substantial slowdown in growth in and after 1978. Outputs of chemical fertiliser, synthetic rubber, synthetic and artificial fibres, plastics and resins have either stabilised or grown very slowly since 1978 and in 1980 were only 50 — 66 per cent of the targets established in the five-year plan. Despite the reduced oil availability annual plan targets for petrochemicals were only marginally revised downwards and these were fulfilled by only 60 — 77 per cent. The effect on the balance of payments has been that chemical exports to the West have stabilised at 80 million dollars while fertiliser exports have fallen and imports of potassium fertilisers have increased.[18]

Other industrial sectors have also been adversely affected. A number of statistical problems make it difficult to 'audit' Romanian plan fulfilment with any degree of certainty. It is however possible to discern a progressive decline in the degree of fulfilment of most plan indicators with many targets underfulfilled by 25 per cent. Annual plan targets were revised downwards by only small amounts and were also substantially underfulfilled.

Measurement of the Cost of Plan Failure

So it seems that the relatively poor performance of Romanian industry in the sixth five-year plan was largely due to the failure to achieve planned outputs of primary energy and raw materials (basically coal, lignite, and oil), which resulted in the reduction in feedstocks going to petrochemical production and in electricity supply. This created bottle-necks in industrial supplies and the underutilisation of industrial capacity (notably in the petroleum refining and petrochemical industries) which resulted in increased underfulfilment of planned industrial outputs as the plan progressed. Constraints on hard currency earnings, compounded by the breakdown of bilateral contracts with traditional oil suppliers and increased crude oil prices, prevented Romania from importing sufficient quantities of crude oil to compensate for domestic shortfalls and resulted in substantial hard currency deficits.

This section will attempt to disaggregate and quantify the foreign exchange cost to Romania of the failure to fulfil primary energy targets by converting unfulfilled energy plans to oil equivalent and multiplying by the average price paid by Romania for imported oil in each of the years in question. This will be compared with an estimate to the cost to Romania of remaining outside the CMEA energy supply network. The first calculation is subject to the criticism that it does not measure the true cost to Romania of unattained energy targets as Romania did not in practice replace all shortfalls by imports but cut back on domestic electricity and petrochemical production, and that it does not reflect the marginal cost of oil imports.

Although the calculation does not give an exact indication of the amount of foreign exchange expended to meet planned production targets it does indicate the amount of oil Romania could have delivered to the petrochemical industry while maintaining planned electricity production for an identical foreign exchange cost. It also gives further insights into Romanian strategy which help to evaluate planners' responses to problems and to analyse the strategy of the seventh five-year plan (1981–5). These estimates are shown in Table 5.7. The principal conclusions can be summarised as follows:

(1) The cost of unfulfilled domestic energy targets is approximately equivalent to Romania's surplus/deficit on 'oil account' (i.e. if domestic energy targets had been realised the value added to exported oil products would have compensated for domestic consumption of crude oil). Had this strategy been maintained, Romania would have isolated itself from the impact of major changes in world oil prices and would have

been affected only by changes in refining margins. A similar analysis would apply to any additional crude oil imports required for the petrochemical industry. The failure to meet domestic energy targets therefore resulted in a vicious circle in which domestic energy demand resulted in Romania becoming a net oil importer with all the resulting problems.

(2) Energy losses resulting from unfulfilled coal and lignite plans are larger in all years (except 1979) than those resulting from unfulfilled oil and gas plans (although the latter are considerably affected by the overfulfilment of gas supplies). The credibility of plans in the mining sector is suspect in view of the ambitious targets established for lignite production at the outset of the plan, and the failure to adjust them in the light of labour disturbances. The establishment of even more ambitious lignite targets in the period 1981-5 make this plan seem similarly unrealistic.

(3) The failure to meet planned energy targets was most severe in 1979 and 1980 − just when the terms on which Romania obtained imported crude oil deteriorated. The average price of Romanian crude oil imports increased 2½ times between 1978 and 1980 as the general increase in world oil prices was aggravated in Romania's case by the loss of favourable contracts with Iran following the fall of the Shah. The foreign exchange cost of failing to meet domestic energy plans would only have been $0.5 billion and $0.6 billion in 1979 and 1980 respectively at the price Romania paid for crude oil in 1978. Consequently $1 billion of the hard currency cost to Romania of the substitutions involved in compensating for underfulfilment of domestic energy plans can be attributed to price changes on world markets and external factors.

(4) The cost to Romania of her isolation from Soviet oil supplies (and the implicit subsidies) is substantial and has probably reached a minimum of $1 billion per annum in 1980. Table 5.7 row 10 provides an estimate of the cost Romania would have paid for imported crude oil at intra-CMEA prices. Row 11 provides an estimate of the price savings to Romania under the unlikely assumption that all her oil imports had been met in this fashion, while row 12 provides an estimate of savings resulting from the more probable assumption that 8 million tons per annum had been provided at intra-CMEA prices. (This volume is below the amount provided to any other East European CMEA country. Furthermore, although Romania received 1,469,000 tons from the USSR in 1980 the cost of 210 million roubles indicates that the price paid approximated to the world market price.)[19] It is,

however, reasonable to suppose that the estimated $1 billion resulting from higher prices on world markets is a substantial underestimate of the real cost to the Romanian economy of its isolation. As shown above (p. 109) Soviet practice in CMEA has not been to demand either full payment in respect of price rises that have taken place in CMEA nor to demand payment in hard goods that can be sold in the West. These factors would substantially raise the cost to Romania of her isolation from CMEA energy supplies.

The Seventh Five-year Plan (1981–5) and Prospects[20]

The major targets of the seventh five-year plan indicate an awareness of the effects of overtaut planning in 1976–80. Proposed growth rates for most aggregates are below those achieved in 1976–80 (see Appendix A) and electricity output which had been planned to reach 90 billion kilowatt hours in 1985 according to the Draft Directives approved at the Twelfth Party Congress in 1979 were reduced to 82.5 billion kilowatt hours in the Final Plan Law. As a result industrial output targets in the Plan Law have also been revised below those in the initial Directives. The Plan Law envisages a more efficient use of resources than the initial Directives which is reflected in a higher rate of reduction of expenditure per 1,000 lei of output and an improvement in the ratio of net to gross industrial output. Furthermore, Ceausescu has indicated that investment priority will be given to the completion of work in progress and the elimination of investment scatter.

The planned energy strategy however appears to be almost identical to that underlying the sixth five-year plan and must give considerable grounds for concern. Lignite production is planned to increase from the 27.1 million tons obtained in 1980 to 73.6 million tons in 1985. According to the original directives this would permit 55 per cent of electricity generation to come from hard fuels while the proportion generated by oil and gas would fall to 20 per cent.

Table 5.5 indicates that this implies a reduction in the volume of electricity generated by oil and gas to 18 billion kwh from the achieved level of 36 billion kwh in 1980, in turn implying a reduced demand for oil and gas in this sector of approximately 5 million tons of oil equivalent below the level required in 1980. The Plan also allows for a slight growth of crude oil output to 12.5 million tons in 1985 which, it is argued, would permit the quantity of crude processed to remain at the 1980 level. (Subsequent reports that crude imports will be limited to

12.5 million tons per annum indicate a lower refining figure.)[21] However, according to Ceausescu, 'raising the degree of chemicalisation' will permit the output of plastics to grow by 70 per cent, synthetic fibres by 80 per cent and synthetic rubber by 60 per cent while fertiliser output will double over the actual 1980 level to 5 million tons in 1985. Surplus is to be restored to the balance of payments by an annual growth of exports of 15.9 per cent compared with 11.9 per cent for total turnover (in constant prices).

The strategy of the plan depends heavily, therefore, on Romania reducing domestic consumption of oil and raising the degree of value added per unit of crude input by increasing the output of petrochemicals, which would enable Romania to compensate for past price increases and restore approximate balance to the 'oil account' so that import price increases would be roughly offset by improved product prices. Both the demand and supply side of the strategy appear to be highly ambitious. Exports of chemicals are planned to treble and exports of chemicals and machinery will constitute 60 per cent of all exports. Romania is currently producing petrochemicals which are subject to CMEA specialisation agreements (for which prices are based on subsidised crude) and it is therefore unlikely that Romania either intends or would be able to expand exports in this sector. Consequently the bulk of the increase must be intended for western markets, implying substantial increases to these areas. However, the western markets for many of the products Romania exports (Ammonia, Methanol, Butanes, Xylenes and Soda Ash) are currently highly competitive and Romania appears to have been obtaining prices in the range of 8–22 per cent below the average EEC price.[22] Romania's exports of these commodities are at present insignificant and although this leads to the possibility of high relative growth rates being achieved, the prospect of a sufficiently high absolute growth must be doubtful. Romania's other major items of exports to industrial economies are mainly industrial consumer goods in which clothing, footwear and furniture predominate, while she also exports some quantities of steel products. These are all items for which competition on world markets is severe, particularly from Third World countries, and Romania may be forced to maintain diplomatic initiatives for recognition as a less-developed country in order to obtain import preferences.

On the supply side Romania's energy strategy depends substantially on trebling the output of lignite the majority of which is to be produced in areas where serious labour disturbances have been experienced on several occasions in the last four years. The five-year plan for

1976-80 proposed a 2.5 fold increase in lignite output whereas a growth of only 37.5 per cent was achieved.[23] A similar performance in the next five-year plan, even assuming all other energy targets are fulfilled, would result in an energy shortfall of the order of 6 million tons of oil equivalent per annum (or $1.5 billion per annum at 1981 prices). Even a doubling of lignite growth would result in substantial energy deficiencies which would require Romania to engage in a combination of domestic electricity cuts and imports of crude oil purely for domestic consumption. The implications of this are serious both for Romania and the West and could be an indication of relations that may prevail with other East European economies towards the end of the decade. Essentially, the apparent complementarity of interests that prevailed in relations between Eastern and Western Europe will be increasingly replaced by competitiveness as Romania competes to import additional quantities of crude oil and raw materials from hard currency sources and to pay for them by increased exports to hard currency markets. Under these circumstances the extension of any favourable loan conditions in the form of subsidised credits, official government supports etc. is likely to operate to the detriment of western producers.

Finally, three possible outcomes for the future are suggested. Certain policies will be common to all scenarios including a slow-down in the rate of industrial growth, attempts to cut back on the domestic concumption of energy and to boost the production of domestic energy sources, increases in prices of consumer goods including foodstuffs, attempts to reschedule debts and obtain further credits from the West, and attempts to obtain bilateral contracts with energy suppliers (both Middle East and CMEA). The scenarios differ largely by the degree to which one policy may predominate over another which may depend more on political than economic factors.

Outcome 1

Consists basically of an attempt to continue current policies involving the simultaneous pursuit of the policies outlined above with no single aspect predominant. The situation would not be unlike that prevailing in Poland before August 1980 but would probably involve a harder line towards the consumer. Industrial priorities would be maintained although the rate of growth of investment would be lower than in previous years. Those aspects of the 1978 reform that were primarily aimed at reducing energy consumption would be continued but otherwise economic planning would remain highly centralised with priority of energy supplies going to industrial outputs. Consumption will not be stimulated, domestic prices will move upwards and tough measures to enforce labour discipline may be required. Attempts would be made to reschedule existing debts and obtain lower cost finance from official agencies while bilateral approaches involving the supply of machinery and equipment to OPEC countries will be pursued vigorously (as outlined in Outcome 2).

Outcome 2

Would consist of a greater level of diplomatic and economic initiatives involving non-CMEA nations. Priority would be given to securing oil supplies on favourable terms which could involve advances to China as well as attempts to secure bilateral contracts with OPEC nations. The damage to oil installations caused by the Iran/Iraq war opens considerable prospects for Romania to supply oil equipment in exchange for crude oil, while initiatives with Libya remain a strong possibility. A further form of co-operation which has been pursued with relatively little success with Kuwait may now be pursued with increased vigour: Romania would use her surplus refining capacity to refine Middle East oil and return products to supplying countries either for a fee or for payment in crude. Other policies to obtain hard currencies would involve sales to Third World countries and direct appeals to Western governments for additional credits and the lifting of any marketing restrictions. To be fully effective in the long run these policies could involve the full implementation of the reform process announced in March 1978 including replacing global output targets with economic indicators and introducing world prices directly into enterprise cost and revenue calculations in order to stimulate a more economic use of raw materials and hopefully to increase marketing incentives. A considerable degree of industrial restructuring would be necessary which may involve closing down uneconomic plants, some of which may be of recent construction. Such a policy is bound to carry with it the risk of social problems due to frictional unemployment although the potential demand for labour in the economy as a whole is likely to remain high.

A further corollary of this policy may be the need to shift investment away from heavy industry towards the production of consumer goods and in particular towards agriculture in order to restimulate agricultural exports, which will also require additional agrarian reforms.

Outcome 3

Involves a re-appraisal of the costs of Romania's independent strategy and re-establishment of closer links with CMEA, involving greater participation by Romania in CMEA integration projects, particularly those involving energy and petrochemicals. This would involve Romania accepting several policies involving joint-planning in CMEA and could also involve the curtailment of certain investment proposals and possibly even the closure of plant. It is difficult to see what other economic concessions Romania could make that would be sufficient to encourage the USSR to provide oil to Romania at heavily subsidised intra-CMEA prices.

In the final analysis Romania may find a greater degree of economic complementarity from supplying foodstuffs to the USSR in exchange for supplies of oil and gas than can be obtained in East-West trade. Although this appears to imply a Romanian capitulation in its dispute with the more industrialised members of CMEA, it could be argued that the level of industrial development already attained is greater than that which would have resulted from initial Romanian participation in Khrushchev's original co-operation proposals.

Outcome One appears to be the most probable of those indicated although this could be considered the least satisfactory both from its impact on the Romanian economy and Romanian consumption levels and carries with it a strong possibility of expanding deficits leading to renewed crises. Outcome Two may be considered the most attractive to the West from a political viewpoint (particularly to those who wish to see the Soviet Union discomfited) but may be the least attractive to the West from an economic viewpoint. In particular, Western Europe would be required to make considerable concessions for Romanian industrial goods to be sold in markets that are already depressed or to open up agricultural markets to Romania at the same time as the EEC is enlarging to admit countries with a similar production profile which may lead to further disagreements over agricultural policy.

Finally, it could be argued that Outcome Three, which may appear politically the least attractive to all concerned, may possess the greatest long-term logic.

Notes

1. International Monetary Fund. International Financial Statistics October 1981.

2. For Plan Targets see Andreas C. Tsantis and Roy Pepper, 'Romania: the Industrialisation of an Agrarian Economy under Socialist Planning' (The World Bank, Washington, 1979) (henceforth referred to as World Bank), p. 186. Plan Fulfilment: Communiqué on the Fulfilment of the Single-National Plan of Socio-Economic Development of the Socialist Republic of Romania in 1976–1980

(Agerpress, Bucharest, January 1981) (subsequently referred to as Communiqué 1976–80).

3. Communiqué 1976–80, p. 37.

4. Neal Ascherson, 'The Polish August' (Penguin Books, 1981), p. 246.

5. Communiqué 1979, see note 2 above.

6. For a fuller discussion of the reforms see Alan Smith, The Romanian Industrial Enterprise in Ian Jeffries (ed.), 'The Industrial Enterprise in Eastern Europe' (Praeger, 1981). For a discussion of workers' committees see Daniel N. Nelson in Soviet Studies (October 1980).

7. N. Ceausescu, Speech, June 1980 (Agerpress, Bucharest).

8. All figures taken from Anuarul Statistic al RSR 1978.

9. For details and original sources see Alan Smith, Romanian Economic Relations with the EEC, 'Jahrbuch der Wirtschaft Osteuropas', Band 8 (Munchen, 1979).

10. World Bank, p. 120.

11. The original analysis of the dispute is provided by J.M. Montias in 'Economic Development in Communist Romania' (MIT Press, Cambridge, Mass., 1967).

12. N. Ceausescu, Speech, October 14 (Agerpress, Bucharest).

13. World Bank, p. 390.

14. Plan details from: Law on the Adoption of the Single National Plan for Socio-Economic Development 1976–1980 (Agerpress, Bucharest, July 1976). Supplemented by M. Manescu, Romania's Socio-Economic Development 'Revue Romaine des Sciences Sociales'.

15. World Bank, p. 340.

16. World Bank, p. 341.

17. Details of fulfilment taken from Anuarul Statistic various years and Plan Communiqué referred to in notes 2 and 5.

18. Estimated from OECD data.

19. Volume from N. Ceausescu Speech, June 1980 – value from Vneshnyaya Torgovlya za SSSR 1980.

20. Plan targets calculated from: Law on the Single National Plan for Romania's Social and Economic Development over the 1981–85 period (Agerpress, Bucharest, July 1981). Supplemented by speeches by Ilie Verdet (Prime Minister) and N. Ceausescu (Agerpress, Bucharest, July 1981).

21. Scinteia, August 1981.

22. OECD, East-West Trade in Chemicals, (Paris, 1980) passim.

23. Overstatement of Plan Fulfilment at the Oltenia Mining Combine and other illegalities and violations are currently the subject of an official enquiry. See N. Ceausescu, Speech, July 1981 (Agerpress).

Table 5.1: Romanian Foreign Trade (millions of valuta lei – current prices 1980 figures recalculated in valuta lei)

| | Trade with Non-socialist Countries | | | | | | | | |
| | Industrial market | | | Developing Countries | | | Annual balance | Estimated cumulative balance | Estimated indebtedness million $ US |
	Exports	Imports	Balance	Exports	Imports	Balance			
1960	917	913	+4	246	132	+114	+188	+118	
1965	1630	2148	-518	437	351	+86	-432	-2031	
1967	2616	4360	-1744	1021	396	+625	-1119	-2092	
1970	3543	4646	-1103	1111	776	+335	-776	-5793	
1973	6591	7462	-871	2375	1712	+663	-208	-6988	1495
1974	10182	12436	-2254	3544	3126	+418	-1836	-8824	2483
1975	9291	11221	-1930	5042	3764	+1278	-652	-9476	2449
1976	10585	10966	-381	5918	5574	+344	-38	-9514	2528
1977	10538	12801	-2262	7398	5511	+1887	-376	-9890	3388
1978	12041	15801	-3760	6628	6865	-237	-3997	-13887	4992
1979	16570	17589	-1019	7537	11340	-3803	-4822	-18709	6700
1980	20055	18541	+1515	12927	20946	-8019	-6504	-25213	9000

Notes: a. Fob; Fob.
b. Country of purchase and sale up to 1978: country of origin and destination after 1978.
c. Industrial market recalculated to include Greece, Spain, Portugal, Turkey.
d. 1960–71 $ US = 6 lei; 1972 5.53 lei; 1973–7 4.97 lei; 1978 4.47 lei.
Source: Anuarul Statistic. Various issues. Except indebtedness; CIA estimates.

Table 5.2: Product Balances in Trade with all Countries (million valuta lei)

	Machinery and Equipment	Fuels and Raw Materials	Raw Materials of Agricultural Origin – Non Food & Semi-Fabricates	Foodstuffs	Chemicals Fertilisers Rubber	Building Materials	Industrial Consumer Goods	Crude Oil Imports
1960	−591	+260	+111	+715	−196	+68	+49	nil
1965	−1293	−373	+203	+1202	+18	+132	+295	nil
1967	−2940	−592	+248	+2077	−98	+107	+293	nil
1970	−2208	−1066	−57	+1208	−10	+104	+1363	144
1973	−2799	−1611	−613	+2838	+233	+427	+2683	527
1974	−3714	−2902	−952	+2778	+128	+486	+2839	2159
1975	−2496	−4241	−559	+2399	+1136	+446	+3265	1988
1976	−1733	−5066	−242	+2323	+560	+575	+3973	3578
1977	−3484	−5813	−672	+4092	+808	+741	+4432	4075
1978	−4860	−7066	−569	+2411	+672	+458	+4900	5543
1979	−4274	−8434	−975	+1939	+589	+475	+5426	9163
1980	−413	−1380	−850	+1202	+1668	+542	+6558	17100

Notes: Columns 1–7 from Anuarul Statistic.
Column 8 from data given to World Bank and IMF converted to valuta lei.

Table 5.3: Trade with Principal Oil Sources (million valuta lei)

	Exports					Imports				
	1975	1976	1977	1978	1979	1975	1976	1977	1978	1979
Iran	811	928	1053	819	578	891	1506	1466	1083	1617
Iraq	325	157	83	147	290	35	856	1037	1964	4151
Libya	582	566	664	707	510	351	708	453	1149	1315
Total	1718	1051	1800	1673	1378	1277	3070	2956	4196	7083

Source: Annurul Statistics various years.

Table 5.4: Oil, Gas and Coal Production

	1970	1975	1976	1977	1978	1979	1980	1985 Plan
A. Oil (million tons)								
Crude oil Production Plan	13.4	14.6	14.7	14.8	15.1	15.3	15.5	12.5
Actual			14.7	14.7	13.7	12.3	11.5	
Imports	2.2	5.1	8.5	8.8	12.9	14.3	15.9	12.5
Refined product exports	5.4	6.2	7.8	6.7	7.6	7.4	9.2	
Net domestic availability	10.2	13.5	15.4	16.9	19.1	19.2	18.2	25.0
Value ($ billion)								
Product exports		0.54	0.73	0.72	0.91	1.86	2.21	
Crude imports		0.40	0.72	0.82	1.24	2.05	3.82	
Balance		+0.14	+0.01	-0.10	-0.33	-0.19	-1.61	
B. Methane gas production (billion cubic metres)	20.0	27.0	29.8	28.8	29.0	27.2	28.2	31.0
C. Coal production (thousand tons)								
Plan (total)			29.6	33.5	38–41	46–8	53–7	85.6
Actual (total)	27.1	27.1	25.8	26.8	29.3	32.8	35.2	
of which Hard Coal	7.3	7.3	7.1	7.1	7.4	8.1	8.1	12.0
Lignite	19.7	19.7	18.7	19.6	21.8	24.7	27.1	73.6

Sources: Five-year Plan Targets: World Bank pp. 618-19.
1985 Targets: Plan Law for 1981-5.
Oil value data: IMF International Financial Statistics (converted to $).
Actual Production, Exports, Imports: Anurul Statistics various years. Communiqué on Plan Fulfilment for 1980.

Table 5.5: Electricity Production

	1976	1977	1978	1979	1980	Plan data 1980	Plan data 1985	1980 surplus deficit[a] (billion kwh)
Output (billion kwh)								
(a) Planned: 5-year plan	57.5	63.1	65/ 67.7	70/ 73.4	75/ 78.8	75/ 78.8	82.5	−7.5
Annual plan	57.5	63.1	64.5	70.3	72.0			
(b) Actual	58.3	59.9	64.3	64.9	67.5			
Inputs (%)								
Hard Coal	10.6	10.8	9.5	10.6	10.2	44.0	55.0	−15.0
Lignite	15.7	15.0	14.2	16.1	16.3			
Natural Gas	52.9	46.1	41.3	39.2	41.8	33.0	20.0	+10.0
Oil	4.3	10.0	15.9	14.3	10.5			
Hydro	13.9	15.6	16.5	17.5	18.7	18.4	20.0	−1.0
Other	2.6	2.5	2.6	2.3	2.5	4.6	5.0	−1.0

Note. Column eight indicates the surplus deficit between the planned volume to be generated by each input and the estimated actual production in 1980 in billion kilowatt hours.
Sources: See Table 5.4.

Table 5.6: Petrochemicals: Planned and Actual Production 1976–80 (thousand tons)

	1970	1975	1976	1977	1978	1979	1980
1. Chemical Fertilisers							
a. Planned: Five-year			2280	3057	3450–3604	3800–4040	4050–4143
Annual			2280	2882	3100	3513	3797
b. Actual,	895	1729	1869	1981	2461	2522	2451
of which: Potassium	4	34	45	51	79	75	57
Phosphorus	244	404	493	548	660	709	687
Nitrogenous	647	1292	1331	1381	1723	1738	1707
2. Plastics and Resins							
Planned: Five-year	206		512	556	600–675	800–884	1000–1057
Actual		347	465	544	552	516	579
3. Synthetic and Artificial Yarns and Fibres							
Planned: Five-year	77		174	184	191	210–233	310–349
Actual		159	178	184	197	196	206
4. Synthetic Rubber							
Planned: Five-year	61		147	175	180–199	240–260	290–318
Actual		99	95	136	148	149	150

Sources: Five-year Plan Data: World Bank; Annual Plan Communiqués.
Fulfilment: Anuarul Statistics, various years, Statisticheskii Yezhegodnik SEV, Plan Communiqués.
Note: The annual output targets established in the Five-year Plan for 1978, 1979 and 1980 were given as ranges. The first figure indicates the bottom of the range, the second the top of the range.

Table 5.7: Estimated Cost of Failure to Fulfil Energy Plan Targets in Sixth Five-year Plan

	1976	1977	1978	1979	1980
Overfulfilment/underfulfilment in tons of oil equivalent					
Lignite	-0.57	-0.99	-1.56	-2.25	-3.36
Coal	-0.16	-0.35	-0.39	-0.31	-0.51
Sub total	-0.73	-1.34	-1.95	-2.56	-3.87
Crude oil	–	-0.15	-1.40	-3.00	-4.00
Natural gas	+2.31	+0.77	+1.69	+0.31	+1.08
Sub total	+2.31	+0.62	+0.29	-2.69	-2.92
Total	+1.58	-0.72	-1.66	-5.25	-6.79
Estimated gain/loss ($ billion)	+0.13	-0.07	-0.16	-0.75	-1.63
Total actual cost of crude imports	0.72	0.82	1.24	2.05	3.82
Estimated intra CMEA cost	0.42	0.54	0.91	1.40	1.77
Estimated savings to Romania if					
All oil at CMEA price	0.30	0.28	0.33	0.65	2.05
8 million tons per annum at CMEA price	0.28	0.25	0.20	0.36	1.03

Notes. a. Calorific values used for conversions. Coal 4 150 kilocalories per kg; Lignite 1785 Kc per kg; Crude oil 10.6 million Kc per metric tonne. From World Bank p. 343.
b. Data on Crude oil imports from Table 5.4. Estimated gain and loss prorated according to actual price paid for crude oil imports.
c. Intra-CMEA price based on estimates of prices paid from volumes and values from Soviet and partners' data converted to $.
d. All value figures (rows 9-12) in $ US billion of current years.

Appendix A: Major Economic Indicators 1976–80 (% growth rates)

	1976	1977	1978	1979	1980
National income	10.5	8.5	7.6	6.2	2.5
Gross industrial output	11.2	12.7	9.0	8.0	6.5
Gross agricultural output	17.2	-0.9	2.4	5.0	-5.0
Investment	8.2	13.6	15.9	4.1	3.1
Number of employees	4.1	2.8	3.2	3.3	2.2
Industrial labour productivity	8.8	9.3	7.1	6.4	4.2
Retail sales	8.6	6.4	11.5	5.8	6.4

Sources: Anuarul Statistics, various years. Communiques on Plan Fulfilment.

Appendix B: Plan Indicators and Fulfilment of Fifth, Sixth and Seventh Five-year Plans (growth rates)

	1971-5				1976-80				1981-5		
	Plan A	Plan B	Actual		Plan A	Plan B	Actual		Plan A	Plan B	
	Five years	Five years	Five years	Annual average	Five years	Five years	Five years	Annual average	Five years	Five years	Annual average
Social product	na	na	65	10.5	47–54	50–7	39.6	6.9	33.5–37.5	34.3	6.1
National income	45–50	69–76	70.6	11.3	54–61	61–68.5	41.5	7.2	38–43	41.1	7.1
Industrial output											
Gross	50–7	69–76	84.7	12.9	54–61	62–70	57.4	9.5	47–54	44.0	7.6
Net	–	–	–	–	–	–	62.0	10.1	54–61	52.4	8.8
Agricultural output[a]	28–31	36–49	25.4	6.5	25–34	28–44	26.4	4.8	24–27.5	24.4–27.4	4.5–5.0
Investment[a]	48–53	65	68.3	11.5	65–72	83.4	67.5	10.9	30–5	28.9	5.2
Employees	7.8–9.8	19.6	23.3	4.3	16–19	16–9.2	16.5	3.1	10.5–12.5	7.9	1.5
Labour productivity											
Industry	37–40	42	37	6.4	38–42	50–53.8	40.4	7.0	40–43.5	40.4	7.0
Construction	27–31	35	46.1	7.9	50–6	50–56.9	45.8	7.8	30–5	30.1	5.4
Reduction in material expenditure per 1000 lei output	6–7	11–12	9.2	–	6.5–7.0	8.5–9.5	6.3		5.5–6.0		
Retail sales[b]	30–5	40–7	48.3	8.2	40–5	45–47.5	46.2	8.0	20–3	26.6	4.8
National income per head	37–42		62.6	10.2	20–5	20–9	29.0	5.2		18.0	3.4

Notes. A. Directives.

B. Plan Law.

a. Growth in five-year plan period over preceding plan period.

b. All figures in current prices.

Prices: 1971–5 all figures in comparable prices except Retail Sales. 1976–80 plan targets in fixed (1963) prices, except Retail Sales. Outputs in current prices following 1977 price review.

6 DID SOVIET ECONOMIC GROWTH END IN 1978?*

Michael Ellman

What happened to the national income [of Hungary] in 1974? At current prices it showed an increase of 4.7 per cent, while at comparable prices the growth became already 7 per cent ('Statistical Yearbook 1974', Budapest, 1975, pp. 73–4). Instead of 'deflation', 'inflation' of the index occurred. What was the real growth? In my opinion it was at most 1–2 per cent in 1974. And this would have been good to know at that time.

A. Bródy (1980, p. 196)

The purpose of this chapter is to assess the macro-economic performance of the Soviet economy in 1979–81. Many people have the idea, carefully fostered by certain Soviet official statistics, that during the current world economic crisis the USSR has continued growing, albeit at slower rates than in the past. In this chapter Soviet statistics on the performance of the economy in 1979–81 will be critically assessed in order to establish whether or not this is true. The chapter has a tentative character and its conclusions should not be treated as definitely proven.

The Soviet official statistics for the growth of national income are set out in Table 6.1.

Casual inspection of Table 6.1 shows three important things. First, for three of the five years for which both figures are available, the figure for the rate of growth of NMP produced in comparable prices is higher than that for the rate of growth of NMP produced in current prices. This implies that the price level is falling. As a statement about the Soviet price level in 1976–8 this is clearly absurd. Clearly, some kind of statistical trickery is going on to produce this result, as is in fact implied by the Hungarian economist Bródy in the quotation which heads this chapter. Already ten years ago, Becker (1972, p. 109) suggested that 'The implicit price deflator of NMP may be downwards biased'. Since then, inflationary pressures in the USSR have greatly increased and, for the period from 1976 onwards, Becker's cautious 'may be' can be replaced by the more robust 'is obviously'. Not only Hungarian and US economists are in the sceptical camp. In his

Table 6.1: Annual Rates of Growth of Soviet Net Material Product[a] According to Soviet Official Statistics (in % p.a.).

Year	NMP produced		NMP used[b]	
	Current prices	Comparable prices	Current prices	Comparable prices
1976	4.9	5.3	4.7	5
1977	4.5	5.0	4.0	3.5
1978	4.2	4.8	4.5	4
1979	2.8	2.5	2.4	2
1980	4.1	3.5[c]	4 [d]	3.8[e]
1981[f]	n.a.	n.a.	n.a.	3.2

Notes: a. 'Net material product' is the western term for what in the USSR is referred to as 'national income'. It is calculated according to the MPS (material product system) method rather than the SNA (system of national accounts) method used in the West and therefore is not comparable with 'national income' as calculated in the West. It is roughly true that GDP = NMP + non-material services (e.g. education) + depreciation + rent. An alternative formulation is that it is roughly true that NMP = GDP − (non-material services + depreciation + rent).
b. According to official explanations, the difference between NMP produced and NMP used is caused by losses and the foreign trade balance. The foreign trade balance which adds to or substracts from NMP produced to yield NMP used, is valued in import prices for an import surplus and in export prices for an export surplus. See M. Kaser, A survey of the national accounts of Eastern Europe, 'Income and Wealth IX' (1961), p. 162.
c. For 1980, presentation of the data changed, and differs from previous years. Unlike previous years, in its detailed figures of NMP (p. 379), 'Nark. hoz. 1980' gives no figures for the growth of NMP produced in comparable prices. The figure in the table comes from 'SSSR v tsifrakh v 1980g', p. 23. There is no explicit statement there that the figure is in comparable prices.
d. Calculated from rounded figures and therefore subject to rounding errors.
e. For 1980, presentation of the data changed, and differs from previous years. Unlike previous years, in its detailed figures on NMP (p. 196), 'SSSR v tsifrakh' for 1980 does not give a figure for 1980 growth in NMP used in comparable prices. The figure in the table comes from the summary section of the booklet (p. 23). There is no explicit statement there that the figure given is in comparable prices.
f. At the time of writing, neither statistical handbook for 1981 was yet available. The one figure in the row comes from the official plan fulfilment report for 1981, 'Pravda' 24.1.82.
Source: The statistical handbooks 'Narodnoe khozyaistvo SSSR' and 'SSSR v tsifrakh' for the relevant years. For 1981, see note f.

well-known study of the national income of the USSR, Vainshtein (1969, pp. 133-7) rejected the idea that in 1958-67 the NMP used in comparable prices grew faster than the NMP in current prices (i.e. that the Soviet price level fell in 1958-67) as is shown in official statistics. He suggested that this ignored some significant open and hidden[1] price increases.

Secondly, the change in the publication procedures for the 1980 data is suspicious. The decision by the Soviet Central Statistical Administration to discontinue publication of data in a series which hitherto has been published annually, is normally a sign that the underlying situation has deteriorated sharply and that the data, if published, would be embarrassing. For example, the last 'Nark.hoz.' to contain data on prices at the collective farm markets (which up till then had been regularly published) was that for 1968. Since then, such a table has been simply missing from the annual statistical handbook. The actual figure for 1969 (the first year in which the non-publication policy was applied) seems to have been an increase of 8.5 per cent (Severin, 1979, p. 27), a large amount for the 'inflation free' Soviet Union. Subsequently there have been further significant increases (which no doubt explain why publication of this series has not been recommenced). Similarly, publication of infant mortality statistics ended in 1974 (Davis and Feshbach, 1980, p. 3). The reason, clearly, was that Soviet infant mortality was rising and that to acknowledge this in published official statistics would violate the important Soviet principle of 'partymindedness'. ('Partymindedness' means that all decisions — including those related to the publication of statistical data — should be made on the basis of whether or not they advance the goals and interests of the Communist Party of the Soviet Union.) Hence it seems reasonable to conclude that the decision of the Soviet Central Statistical Administration to downgrade, for 1980, the detailed information on NMP in comparable prices, hitherto published annually, was intended to reduce the attention paid to this — currently very depressing — statistic. It will be interesting to see whether this change in the arrangement of the data in the statistical handbooks continues in 1981. In a period of inflation, it is of course the figures in comparable prices and not in current prices that are important for evaluating growth. Suppose, for example, that in the UK in 1981 inflation was 12 per cent and growth −2 per cent. Then the statistic that in current prices the national income rose 10 per cent, while it might impress an economist from some distant country (if the published price index was massaged and the data on national income in comparable prices were dropped from the section on national income statistics of the statistical annuals) would not really be very impressive, even if Ministers made speeches about this important achievement.

Thirdly, the figures for 1979 and for the three year period 1979–81 show a sharp deterioration compared with 1978 and the three year period 1976–8. In 1979, NMP used in comparable prices grew, according to Table 6.1, at only half the rate of 1978 or the average for

1976-8. In the three years 1979-81, NMP used in comparable prices grew, according to Table 6.1, at only three-quarters of the rate in the previous three years.

The three factors considered above, taken together, suggest that from the standpoint of economic growth, 1979 was the beginning of a period in which performance deteriorated sharply compared to previous years.

Should the information that NMP used in comparable prices rose by 3 per cent per annum in 1979-81 be accepted, or is it affected by bias in the NMP implicit price deflator? The views of Bródy, Becker and Vainshtein have already been cited. More recently, the Soviet economist Volkonsky (1981, p. 98, italics added) has more or less repeated the argument of Schroeder (1972, pp. 307-12). 'In our statistics', he wrote, 'price indices are calculated from a fixed list of goods. Such indices in fact reflect only price changes resulting from changes in the official prices for particular goods. With fixed price lists, however, it is possible for a significant growth in the indices for a group of prices and for the general level of prices to take place, as a result of alterations in the volumes of output of the different goods within a group, as a result of the introduction of new goods, as a result of quality changes etc. Such a "hidden" growth of prices is not insignificant both from the point of view of the efficiency of the planned management of production and also from the standpoint of the psychology of consumers.'

The arguments put forward by Becker, Bródy, Vainshtein, Schroeder and Volkonsky suggest that all the official figures for Soviet macroeconomic magnitudes in comparable prices are biased upwards due to deficiencies in the ways that the price indices are calculated. Hence the official figures for the level of NMP used in comparable prices in the years 1979, 1980 and 1981 are probably too high. There is an additional factor, however, which suggests that the degree of exaggeration is rising over time and that the 'law of equal cheating'[2] does not apply in 1979-81. In this period inflationary tension in the USSR rose sharply relative to the early 1970s. Both open and suppressed inflation increased. Hence in 1979-81, in all probability, not only the official figures for the level of NMP used in comparable prices, but also for the rate of growth of NMP used in comparable prices, are biased upwards.

Open price increases in state retail trade in the USSR have taken place on four occasions in recent years, namely 5 January 1977, 1 March 1978, 1 July 1979 and 15 September 1981. The first price increases affected carpets, silk fabrics, cut glass, taxi fares, etc. The second affected petrol, spare parts for cars, coffee and jewellery. The third affected cars, jewellery, food served in restaurants and cafes in the evening, carpets, beer drunk in beer halls etc, furs and furniture. The last affected jewellery, cut glass, carpets, furs, leather goods, china, high quality woollen and downy shawls, some suites of furniture, petrol, boats, alcoholic drinks and tobacco goods. Although most of the goods in these lists can be regarded as luxury goods rather than necessities, their combined effect was no doubt significant. This applies in particular to the large price increases for alcoholic drinks and tobacco goods (officially 17–27 per cent on average) in September 1981 which is bound to have hit living standards sharply. Not only have state retail prices risen significantly in recent years, but so have the prices of a wide range of producer goods, most notably as part of the general revision of the price lists which came into effect on 1 January 1982. This increased, for example, the average price of coal by 42 per cent, that of natural gas by 45 per cent, that of ferrous metal products by 20 per cent, industrial timber by 40 per cent etc.

The increase in suppressed inflation is shown by the following. First, since 1974 prices at the collective farm markets have been rising continuously (Severin, 1979, p. 27).[3] Hence there has been a steady increase in the Holzman indicator of suppressed inflation (Dirksen, 1981).[4] Secondly, shortages worsened in the late 1970s and queues lengthened. For this there is abundant firsthand ('anecdotal') evidence. Thirdly, by the end of 1981, rationing of meat and dairy products was widespread in the USSR. This resulted from the combination of stagnant output, a significant increase in money incomes, high income elasticities of demand for these products, and the attempt to prevent state retail prices rising too much. The latter was no doubt partly a response to fear of a possible spread of the 'Polish disease'. Fourthly, the agricultural subsidies have been increasing significantly. These appear to have risen from about 19 billion roubles in 1978 (4.6 per cent of NMP used) to 25 billion roubles (5.6 per cent of NMP used) in 1980 and 33 billion roubles (7 per cent of NMP used) in 1981.[5]

In a shortage economy it would be useful and sensible to collect and publish statistics on shortages, just as in a market economy it is useful and sensible to collect and publish statistics on unemployment. This has been forcefully argued by the Hungarian economist Kornai (1980, vol A, p. 46) who has observed that, 'A long time passed before the systematic observation and measurement of unemployment was introduced in every capitalist country. In socialist countries the shortage problem has become topical. Sooner or later the systematic measurement of shortage indicators will be organized.' The same point has been argued in a Soviet book ('Planovyi', 1981, p. 185) sponsored by the Central Economic Mathematical Institute of the USSR Academy of Sciences (TSEMI).

At the present time the study of unsatisfied demand is conducted in a clearly unsatisfactory way. The task consists of replacing the episodic recording of unsatisfied demand by the regular supply of these data to the state statistical agencies. The need has arisen to work out special forms for recording unsatisfied demand and to determine scientific methods for the summarising of the data received.

Although, unfortunately, at the present time published Soviet statistics are deficient in indices of shortages, it is to be hoped that in due course the advice of Kornai and TSEMI will be followed and that it will not be necessary to rely on the crude indices used in the previous paragraph.

In the late 1970s the social indicators movement spread to the USSR ('Sovershenstvovanie', 1979, 'Pokazateli', 1980). Hence in the eleventh five-year plan (1981-5) the section on raising living standards of the previous five year plans was transformed into a plan for social development. Accordingly, it would be in keeping with contemporary ideas, both Western and Soviet, about the assessment of Soviet development in 1979-81, to look not only at economic but also at social indicators. One important social indicator is the extent and importance of shortages and queues. Shortages and queues, of course, are a normal feature of the Soviet economy. Indeed, the Hungarian economist Kornai in his famous work 'Economics of Shortage' has developed a whole economic theory about them. As he has noted (ibid., vol. A, p. 134), 'The instantaneous intensity of shortage fluctuates round its normal value, and from time to time may grow particularly severe, which may lead to the sharpening of social and economic tensions'. 1979-81 was one such period in the USSR. A particularly important shortage is that of housing. In 1979-81 the existing severe housing shortage worsened. This can be demonstrated as follows. A standard measure of the housing shortage is the relationship between the number of households and the number of dwellings. For the USSR, official data on household numbers for non-census years are not published. Following Morton (1979, p. 799), however, one can use the number of marriages as a proxy for the increase in household numbers. This is an imperfect measure since it excludes both deaths (which reduce the housing shortage) and any (actual or potential) decline in the average size of households and demolition (which increase it). Nevertheless, in the absence of direct data on household numbers for non-census years it is not too bad a proxy. Morton himself showed that the housing shortage, measured this way, declined in every year between 1961 and 1968, but steadily increased between 1969 and 1977. Data for 1978–80 are now available, and these show that the number of flats completed has continued to be much below the number of marriages. In addition, it is well known that the Soviet mortality situation, notably infant mortality, deteriorated in the early 1970s (Davis and Feshbach, 1980). Although the tighter censorship prevents one from determining precisely what happened to the age-specific death rates in 1979–81, it should be noted that the crude death rate for the population as a whole rose significantly in both 1979 and 1980 ('Nark.hoz.', 1980, p. 31). Most of this increase was probably accounted for by the ageing of the population. Some of it, however, may well have resulted from a worsening of the age-specific death rates, data on which are no longer published.

That the inclusion of social indicators in an assessment of the development of the USSR should worsen the USSR's position relative to the OECD countries would not be entirely surprising. The UN's Economic Commission for Europe has recently carried out a study ('Economic Bulletin for Europe', vol. 31, no. 2, New York, 1980), in which conventional measures of GDP and NMP were replaced by a synthetic index based both on industrial inputs (e.g. steel consumption) and welfare data (e.g. housing space and conditions). This kind of calculation has three advantages for inter-system comparisons of economic growth. First, it removes distortions caused by the differences between the MPS and SNA methods (both systems are measured in the same way). Secondly, it removes distortions caused by the biased price deflators used in the CMEA countries. Thirdly, it removes the artificial advantage which measuring only 'productive' indices and ignoring welfare indicators confers on countries which adopt 'rushed' growth rather than 'harmonious' growth (to use Kornai's terminology). When applied to the USSR and the UK in 1951–73 it led to a sharp reduction in the difference between the two countries in the per capita rate of macro-economic growth (although the difference remained substantial).

Given that the official summary macro-economic data in prices are unreliable, it is interesting to present some physical output data to get a picture of what happened to the Soviet economy in 1979–81. This is done in Table 6.2.

Table 6.2 shows a slow but continuous growth of electricity output,

Table 6.2: Soviet Economy 1979–81, Selected Physical Data

Year	Electricity output (billions of kilowatt hours)	Car output (millions)	No. of flats built[a] (millions)	Oil output including condensate (million tonnes)	Iron ore output (million tonnes)	Timber output (million m³)	Natural gas output (million m³)	Coal output[b] (million tonnes)	Railway freight[c] (million tonnes)	Grain output[d] (bunker output million tonnes)	Meat output[e] (million tonnes)	Whole milk production[f] (million tonnes)	Rate of growth of population (in % p.a.)
1978	1202	1.3	2.1	572	246	284	372	724	3776	237	9.6	24.8	0.9
1979	1238	1.3	1.9	586	242	273	407	719	3688	179	9.6	25.0	0.8
1980	1295	1.3	2.1	603	245	278	435	716	3728	189	9.2	25.3	0.8
1981	1325	1.3	2	609	242	274	465	704	3746	n.a.[g]	9.2	25.7	0.8

Notes: a. The number of flats built in the USSR peaked in 1959 and in 1981 was about one quarter below that level.
b. In Soviet statistical publications there are two figures for coal output, gross and net. The latter is more meaningful from an economic viewpoint, but in the table the former is used. This is to ensure comparability with 1981 for which only the gross figure is yet available.
c. For a good discussion of the economics of Soviet railway freight see V. Selyunin, Nerv Ekonomiki, 'Druzhba Narodov', (1981) no. 11.
d. Soviet grain output statistics measure 'bunker' output rather than 'barn' output. The former exceeds the latter because it includes some moisture content of grain, trash and dirt admixtures, and losses during transport, handling and preliminary storage.
e. Includes offal. The figures in the table are for industrially processed meat, not for total gross output. The latter also fell in 1978–81.
f. i.e. kefir, sour cream ('smetana'), milk products and milk, calculated in milk equivalent. The figures in the table are for industrially processed milk, not for total gross output. In 1978–81 the latter declined by 6 per cent. The reason why the output of industrially processed milk could rise at the same time that total gross output fell is that in this period the extent of marketing and processing of Soviet agricultural production rose.
g. This is another example of the deterioration of Soviet statistical reporting in recent years. No figure is given in the plan fulfilment report for grain output. Instead there is the following revealing sentence, 'State grain resources will provide in full for the supply to the population of bread and bread products'. Soviet grain imports in 1981 were very large.
Source: 'Narodnoe khozyaistvo SSSR v 1980g' (Moscow 1981), and 'Pravda', 24 January 1982.

Table 6.3: Annual Average Rates of Growth of Soviet Net Material Product at Comparable Prices According to Soviet Official Statistics[a]

Year	NMP produced at comparable prices
1951–5	11
1956–60	9
1961–5	7
1966–70	8
1971–5	6
1976–80	4

Note. a. Figures have been rounded to nearest whole number.
Source: 'Narodnoe khozyaistvo SSSR' various years.

stagnation in the car industry and in housing construction, a slow and declining rate of growth of oil output, modest declines in the iron ore and timber sectors, fast growth in natural gas output, a slow but steady decline in coal output, a volume of railway freight that in 1981 was still below the 1978 level, three bad harvests and a decline in the live-stock sector. Summarising, Soviet official statistics in physical terms for 1979-81 give the following picture. In industry the situation varied be-tween slow growth and stagnation. In housing construction there was stagnation. In fuel and raw materials production the situation varied from fast growth via slow growth to stagnation and slow decline. In agriculture the situation varied between sharp decline and gentle de-cline. Railway freight transport formed a national economic bottleneck. Since in 1979-81 the population grew at almost 1 per cent p.a., the per capita picture was still worse.

The reason for this depressing[6] situation was the combination of three bad harvests with a secular trend, extending over more than 30 years, for the rate of growth to fall steadily. The secular trend for Soviet growth to decline is a well known phenomenon which has been discussed recently by Hanson (1981), Brus (1981) and Bergson (1981). It can be seen clearly from the data presented in Table 6.3.

Table 6.3 shows clearly that the rate of growth of Soviet net material product has been falling continuously for thirty years with the exception of a relatively favourable period in the late 1960s.

It is important to note that although the Soviet growth experience in 1979-81 compares unfavourably both with the Soviet past and with economically successful countries such as Japan, it compares quite well with a number of countries. In Poland, the NMP produced fell by about 2 per cent in 1979, 4 per cent in 1980 and 13 per cent in 1981. In the UK, GDP (output measure) rose by about 2 per cent in 1979, but fell by about 3 per cent in 1980 and about 3 per cent in 1981. In the UK, manufacturing was a real disaster area, corresponding to grain in the USSR. In the two years since 1980 and 1981 UK manufacturing output fell by about 14 per cent. By Polish or British standards, the USSR's growth performance was good in 1979-81. The USSR also maintained full employment.

Conclusion

Soviet official statistics make it difficult to form a clear picture of the macro-economic development of the Soviet economy in 1979-81 because of the worsening upward bias resulting from an unsatisfactory price deflator. The available data indicate that it is improbable that there was any significant increase in per capita national income in 1979-81. In addition, certain social indicators, e.g. shortages and queues (in particular for meat, dairy products and housing) and the crude death rate, deteriorated. Hence, it seems reasonable to characterise the period 1979-81 as one of economic and social stagnation. Soviet per capita economic growth does seem to have come to a halt, possibly temporary, in 1978. The stagnation was caused by a combination of the long term tendency for the rate of economic growth to decline, with three bad harvests. This picture is a provisional one and may require revision, either upwards or downwards, as more data become available.

The Soviet stagnation of 1979-81 compares adversely with the Soviet past and with the experience of an economically successful country such as Japan but compares favourably with the experience in the same period of countries such as Poland and the UK.

Notes

* I am grateful to J. Cooper, C. Davis, P. Hanson, M. Kaser, R. Knaack and K.E. Wädekin for helpful comments on, and discussion of, a draft of this chapter.

1. It is customary to distinguish between open, suppressed (or repressed) and hidden inflation. Open inflation, the sort of inflation normal in the West, is an ordinary rise in prices. Suppressed inflation is an excess of demand over supply which is not reflected in official price increases (because prices are controlled by the state) but in increased shortages, lengthening queues, a growing black market, an increasing divergence between the official retail prices and actual transactions prices (including bribes, etc.) and growing subsidies. Hidden inflation is an increase in prices which does not show up in the official index because of statistical trickery, e.g. the introduction of 'new' goods which differ from the old only by

means of their higher prices, etc. (A pioneer in the field of hidden inflation was the UK during World War II. It was imperative for the Government to massage the index since wages were tied to it. In this way wage drift could be combated.)

2. The 'law of equal cheating' is the proposition that, although at any given time Soviet macro-economic output statistics contain a considerable amount of padding, this does not affect measures of the rate of growth since the proportion of padding is probably constant over time. See Nove, 1977, p. 352.

3. Severin only gives data up to 1977, but these prices continued to rise in 1978–81.

4. In his Table 2, the last year for which Dirksen calculates a Holzman index is 1979. Since Dirksen's article was written, the statistical handbook for 1980 has been published, which enables one to calculate a Holzman index for 1980. It is 36, a further increase on the 1979 figure.

5. See 'Finansy SSSR' (1982) no. 1 p. 25, 'Sotsialisticheskaya industriya' (3 July 1981), and 'Argumenty i fakty' (1981) no. 16. The 33 billion roubles are for food subsidies alone. There are also some input subsidies.

6. According to the Party Programme adopted at the 22nd Congress (1961), in 1980 the Soviet NMP would be in the range 720–750 billion roubles. In fact it was only 458.5 (NMP produced, current prices), i.e. only about 63 per cent of the target.

References

Becker, A.S. (1972) National income accounting in the USSR in V.G. Treml and J.P. Hardt (eds.), 'Soviet economic statistics', Durham, North Carolina, USA.
Bergson, A. (1981) Can the Soviet slowdown be reversed?, 'Challenge', November/December.
Bródy, A. (1980) On the discussion about measurement – A rejoinder, 'Acta Oeconomica', vol. 25 nos. 1–2.
Brus, W. (1981) Les conséquences économiques du stalinisme, 'Revue européene des sciences sociales et Cahiers Vilfredo Pareto', vol. xix no. 57.
Davis, C. and Feshbach, M. (1980) 'Rising infant mortality in the USSR in the 1970s', Washington D.C.
Dirksen, E. (1981) The control of inflation? Errors in the interpretation of CPE data, 'Economica', August.
Hanson, P. (1981) Economic constraints on Soviet policies in the 1980s, 'International Affairs', winter 1980–1.
Kornai, J. (1980) 'Economics of shortage', Amsterdam.
Morton, H.W. (1979) The Soviet quest for better housing – an impossible dream? 'Soviet economy in a time of change', Joint Economic Committee, US Congress, Washington D.C., vol. 1.
Nove, A. (1977) 'The Soviet economic system', London.
'Planovyi' (1981) 'Planovyi differentsirovannyi balans dokhodov i potrebleniya naseleniya', Moscow.
'Pokazetali' (1980) 'Pokazateli sotsial'nogo razvitiya i planirovaniya', Moscow.
Schroeder, G.E. (1972) An appraisal of Soviet wage and income statistics, in V.G. Treml and J.P. Hardt (eds.), 'Soviet economic statistics', Durham, North Carolina, USA.
Severin, B.S. (1979) USSR: The All-Union and Moscow collective farm market price indexes, 'The ACES Bulletin', vol. xxi, no. 1, Spring.
'Sovershenstvovanie' (1979) 'Sovershenstvovanie gosudarstvennoi statistiki na sovremennom etape' (Moscow 1979 – 'Materialy vsesoyuznogo

soveshchaniya statistikov').
Vainshtein, A.L. (1969) 'Narodnyi dokhod Rossii i SSSR', Moscow.
Volkonsky, V.A. (1981) 'Problemy sovershenstvovaniya khozyaistvennogo mekhanizma', Moscow.

7 THE WORSENING OF SOVIET ECONOMIC PERFORMANCE

Peter Wiles

The economic situation in the USSR is quite bad, but not so bad as in Britain, or as in Poland before the military coup. It is not at all obvious why there has been this decline from the high growth of the 1960s and early 1970s. Very many factors contribute, including some new positive ones. But it is the ones that we can measure, or think we can measure, statistically that receive most attention. I shall try here to redress that balance, by an unusual degree of reliance on Western journalists and Soviet visitors or refugees.

First, what are the facts of economic growth so far as we can estimate them? I present them in several versions in Table 7.1. It will be observed that my own estimates (item 1b in the table) are gloomier than those of the CIA. They start from these propositions:

1. The official figures for money totals at current prices are as correct as may be (this is what everyone assumes, and I simply assume it too).

2. It is more reliable for an outsider to aim at a price index than at an output index; for even Soviet relative prices have some logic, and resemble relative prices in other countries, while relative outputs differ very widely indeed. The outsider cannot know all the outputs in sufficient detail, but if he knows a reasonable number of prices he has enough information.

3. But we have now two unofficial price indices worked out inside the USSR: for investment machinery and investment construction. They emerge from a duly published and censored literature that strongly criticises the two official indices. The main complaints are against abuse of the special rules for new products; sheer tolerated rises in sums paid; and at the centre an official concentration on a very few favourable series of individual prices when constructing the index.

4. There is no explicitly published Western index of construction costs, but the new unofficial machinery index most reassuringly yields an annual rate of understatement of the official price index equal to that derived from the CIA's workings, which of course do not rest on so much inside knowledge or so many quantitative data.

5. The understatement factors were 3.5 per cent p.a. (i.e. +2.0 per

cent instead of − 1.5 per cent) for machinery and 2.75 per cent p.a. (i.e.
+2.5 per cent instead of −0.25 per cent) for the implicit official index
of construction costs in 1966–76; say 3.0 per cent p.a. for investment
as a whole.

6. Three notorious practices cause the cost of living to be understated; the first two are observed by diplomats and other long-term
foreign residents; the second and the third are openly discussed in the
technical literature but not quantified. First is false labelling, the
description of an old low-quality product as a new higher-quality one
with a higher price. Second is the introduction of genuinely new and
better products at the much higher prices permitted in such cases, and
the subsequent suppression of the much cheaper but only slightly worse
quality. Thirdly, the official compilers at the centre exclude luxuries
and foreign goods (some of which are not luxuries), and pay no attention to the actual price paid over the counter but only to the list price.

7. If the CIA is more or less right on machinery (4. above) it might
be right on the cost of living, which it has also calculated. Anyway, by
this and other exceedingly dangerous methods we arrive at an approximate understatement factor in the cost of living index too: 1.4 per cent
p.a. in 1965–70, 1.6 per cent p.a. in 1970–5, 2.9 per cent p.a. in 1975–
9 (i.e. the index itself rose by 1.9 per cent, 2.1 per cent and 3.4 per
cent instead of 0.5 per cent throughout).

8. Arms, the only category not yet covered, can hardly differ from
investment machinery.

9. So I deflate the Soviet figures for net material product at *current*
prices by an average factor of 3.0 per cent since 1975.

As this is written the figures are not in for 1981. But the harvest has
been bad and Brezhnev's speech of 18 November 1981 was quite
alarmist. Not, I would say, since 1947 has a leader's speech on the
economy been so lavish with the word 'difficulty'. 1981 cannot have
been as good as 1980. Therefore, there has been no per capita growth
in 1979–81 inclusive: a unique event since the war.[1] The same applies
to consumption taken alone (Wiles, Soviet Studies 1982). Moreover
none of this looks like a flash in the pan: there is steadily diminishing
growth since 1950. Let us now list our causative factors.

1. Rising prices as such are surely an effect not a cause of poor
output performance, or maybe something altogether independent. In
inter-enterprise transactions money is 'passive'[2] as it has always been,
and always in adequate supply to finance planned transactions. There
may (a) possibly be a little demand inflation at the edges of this sector,
say in the decentralised purchase of investment goods or even of a few

current local supplies. If so the passive money is becoming active, prices remain sticky but are no longer frozen, and the money is in plentiful supply. So the rising wholesale prices are a sign of goods shortage, as the demanders that bid them up. As under capitalism, rising prices would cause lower output only if (b) there were cost inflation. And this there certainly is, in that machinery and building prices are creeping up under that influence — no doubt because of the wage creep endemic in the Soviet labour market. But I have extreme difficulty in imagining any object, for investment or for current output, duly figuring in the production plan of one enterprise, not being bought by the recipient named in the plan because its planned price had risen. This would be an inversion indeed of the Soviet system, and we would surely have heard of it in the technical press. There remains (c) the possibility of cost inflation through wage-creep combined with stable planned prices. Undoubtedly this is common, and it diverts production from some goods to others more profitable, in a rather venial violation of the enterprise's plan; for too many bonuses hang on the enterprise's fulfilment of its total production plan for that to be deliberately underfulfilled. In this case the bank would come to the rescue as it always did, with a 'short-term' loan that is not in fact repaid. Perhaps the most important thing about all this unplanned inflation is that there are other, very important, definitions of bad economic performance than stagnant output. Inflation, especially cost-inflation and wage creep, is a symptom of the new general social indiscipline, to which we return.

2. Inflation in retail and black markets, where the rouble is 'active' and plays a normal role, is the product of excess demand at fixed prices. Seeing the long queues and the profitability of higher prices, the government certainly began in 1980 to raise the prices of luxuries officially. It has also raised vodka (see below for the social causes) and petrol (because of the world scarcity and the necessity to export). The excess demand has been present for a long time, gradually building up as wages and kolkhozniks' payments are salted away in liquid assets. These comprise deposits in savings banks (R.156.5 md. in December 1980), illegal stocks of gold and foreign currency (no estimate), and rouble cash (a state secret since 1936, but thought to be about R.78 md. in December 1980).[3] The sum of the first and the last falls only a little short of the total annual value of retail trade (R.247.8 md. in the year 1978).

It is very difficult to say whether this is a lot or a little. For instance since houses are so difficult to buy a Russian doesn't need to save to buy one, so his stock of cash weighs heavily on other goods. But since

annuities and private pensions are not on sale, and prices are reasonably
stable, and the real rate of interest is positive, perhaps he is just putting
money by in the savings for his old age? However, we may justly compare Hungary and Poland in 1971:

	billion forints[4]	billion zlotys[4]	billion roubles 1978
Volume of state and private retail trade in goods	150	504.1	247.8
Savings deposits at mid-year	45.2	150.3	123.4
Cash in circulation at mid-year	c.21	63.0	c.63
'Velocity'	2.27	2.36	1.33

Actually this gloomy picture is understated. Legal private capitalists in
Communist countries are forced to use cash and savings banks only. So
much of the high figure in Poland, an inflationary country even then,
was actually only the cash trading reserves of capitalist businesses,
especially private peasants. Again 1971 was the high water mark of
tolerated auxiliary enterprises on Hungarian collective farms. Much too,
in all three countries, is the cash trading reserves of illegal businesses.
So, with a much smaller legitimate private sector, the USSR's liquidity
reserves have not even the function of being a base for enterprise. They
are more simply an overhang in the retail market.

It is also very difficult to distinguish the shortages and queues due to
the simple — and endemic in Soviet-type economies — irrational pricing
of particular goods (here too much, so there is a surplus stock the
consumer cannot see, since it is held by the Ministry of Domestic Trade
in its own warehouses; and there too little, so there is a highly visible
queue) from general excess of demand over supply at current fixed
prices. For in the latter case there will always still be something you
don't have to queue for. Nevertheless when queues lengthen and multi-
ply — as they recently have — there is either increased misallocation of
resources or increased excess demand. With all the very genuine improvements in the techniques and physical equipment of Soviet planning, the latter is overwhelmingly more probable. It becomes quite
certain when we reflect that the overall index of prices is rising. For the
State Committee on Prices has very often indeed lowered certain prices
in order to clear markets or keep the index stable, but it is not doing so
now. On the contrary with the rise in miners' wages (27 per cent in
October 1981; 'The Times', 14 September 1981) it becomes possible to
suggest what we never previously dreamed of: the beginnings of open

inflation, with wages chasing prices chasing wages (but prices never rising enough to eliminate excess demand).

3. The lengthening queues deserve separate mention. Whether incorrect relative prices or too low absolute prices are the cause, to queue is to work; to do extra housework. Standing and waiting take time and are more unpleasant than most money-earning work or normal housework. If the volume of consumer goods increases by 10 per cent we are, say 7 per cent better off (for the marginal utility of income diminishes). But if we originally did 42 hours a week plus 5 hours of queueing, and now it is 42 + 9.7, that is 10 per cent more work, or, say, we are 15 per cent worse off (for the marginal disutility of labour increases). So the orthodox statistics tell us we are better off, and indeed our productivity has risen by 10 per cent (for we still only produce for 42 hours); yet we feel worse off, and not being professors of economics we cannot account for it.[5] The lengthening queues probably explain why the Soviet people are reported as more discontented, and saying they are worse off, though the volume index of consumption per head is stable. They would be better off with less money in their pockets or with much higher prices – but let not the Kremlin try!

4. So far we have given not one solid reason for worsening output performance! The technology gap is an old stand-by, and it is obligatory, alas, to repeat the by now hackneyed story.

R & D is the most important of all sectors for future growth, yet capitalism continues to generate most of the technical progress in the world, since Soviet-type R & D is extremely inefficient, and likely to remain so. This failure is ideologically disastrous; for clearly the superior mode of production is the one that develops most inventions. To begin with 'R', its product being new knowledge or a new machine it is by definition unpredictable, i.e. a prototype. It may not be produced at all; or it may be subtly unexpected, or there may be a surprise by-product – in both cases the producer must find another use. Its cost of production cannot be planned. The specific inputs that make up this cost cannot be predicted; so they cannot be acquired through the usual channels of the command economy but must be organised ad hoc. But this can, constitutionally, only come about through the very topmost channels of command, so informality and corruption play a large role. Over and above these problems, researchers must meet foreigners at conferences and make friends with them. For this they require a quick supply of foreign technical journals, good international telephone links and exit visas. The KGB is very obstructive about all this.

'D' consists in making this prototype commercially workable. In the Soviet system this means persuading the director of an ordinary enterprise to organise the new channels of supply and risk his plan-fulfilment bonus on an untried process. He resists, and even when he has finally got the bugs out of it the next director is almost equally recalcitrant, because he too fears for his bonus. So diffusion is much slower than under capitalism, where all tried innovations are thoroughly welcome as raising profits, and the 'know-how', that last stage in 'D', the actual knowledge of which handle to turn when, is eagerly sought and paid for.

Up-to-date figures, indeed any reliable and well conceived figures, on the technology gap are simply not to be had. But the impression remains that it has been closing slightly. One reason for this impression is the reduced purchases of Western machinery in 1978–81, despite a balance of payments position so favourable that debt had been redeemed. These importations have been somewhat disappointing. One reason is undoubtedly the difficulty of importing know-how, another that the very wasteful Soviet investment process becomes intolerable when machinery prices are so high as in this case — and payable in foreign exchange. But a third is, I suspect, the fast development of native substitutes. Against this, however, Philip Hanson suspects that the domestic R & D establishment has merely become more successfully protectionist.[6]

Fourth, and altogether less speculatively, having caught up is inflationary. All the large and obvious improvements having been made, only the more costly and less effective ones remain. Also, and above all, having caught up slows down your growth: that is, the declining growth is itself evidence of all-round technical achievement. Such achievement should not, however, have brought growth down to zero.

5. Another good old standby has long been the wastefulness, referred to above, of the investment process. It is above all wastefully lengthy. Gestation periods are *normed*, ambitiously, at round about best Western practice. Wearily experienced, the planners *plan* them for longer. The *actual* time taken is longer still, and the reason is the unusual inefficiency and extreme overloading of the construction industry. This, then, 'freezes' capital in that half-finished projects have already cost a lot but still produce nothing.

Another 'good old standby' reason is the mere irrationality of capital allocations. There is still no basic rate of return operating throughout the economy, to form a common point of departure for rational cost benefit calculations (J. Giffen, Soviet Studies, 1981). The procedures are, though now expressly formalised, still so vague and arbitrary that any project can be pushed through by a powerful individual, say a regional Party secretary.

But such reasons cannot explain declining performance, only bad performance. Have actual design, construction and running-in periods, then become still longer recently? Each project is a prototype, so good comparable statistics are extremely hard to come by. But Mr P.D. Podshivalenko, a vice-President of the Stroibank,[7] gives us persuasive evidence that the situation has slightly improved. And project criteria have certainly not remained as irrationally wasteful as under Stalin. On this compare especially point 6.

6. An altogether better, if more prosaic, reason is diminishing returns, the rising cost of natural resources. This is very obvious in oil, where calculations exist: the long-run marginal cost of oil has risen ten times since 1974 (Wiles, 1982). This means about 10 times as much investment cost per barrel from a new well; a development simultaneously inflationary and growth-reducing. It is reasonable to infer similar rises in coal and natural gas. However, the weight of this in the total economy must be exaggerated. In 1971 the three sectors absorbed about R. 5.5 md. in gross fixed investment, or 18.3 per cent of the industrial total. In 1979 the figures were R. 10.9 md. and 23.4 per cent; and the fuel was forthcoming. This is no catastrophic deterioration.

Nor are renewable natural resources in much better case. Agriculture is of course the big item here. In 1960 it took directly 13 per cent of all investment where industry took 36 per cent. In 1971 and again in 1980 it took about 20 per cent while industry took about 35 per cent — and much of that was in tractor and fertiliser plants. Yet of course agricultural output grows much slower than industrial. However, this time we face the fact that the switch into the less growth-promoting sector occurred long ago (Nar. Khoz. 1979, pp. 366–8).

Neither of these developments shows any error in Soviet policy — rather the contrary. Nor does the Soviet situation in these respects differ from any capitalist country's. All this must be taken into account before anyone claims increasing inefficiency in Soviet investment.

Agricultural output has of course been particularly disappointing — as usual. Nearly every type of food was in shorter per capita supply in 1980 than in 1979, according to the super-official CMEA Statistical Yearbook 1981; and the year 1981 was even worse (Table 7.1, here). On a merely statistical basis, and without looking deeper into the 'knock-on' effects, a 1 per cent fall in agricultural production reduces GNP by about 0.2 per cent. When the next good harvest comes, agricultural production should rise by about 10 per cent, and so GNP, on that ground alone, by 2.0 per cent.

7. We turn to things that are imponderable themselves or have imponderable effects. The first and greatest of these is the decline of labour discipline. On 20 January 1980 there was an unusual decree on this matter, threatening all sorts of penalties. All journalists' reports confirm the reality which gave rise to this decree — which looks more menacing than it is, and is probably unenforceable. One reason will be the queues in the shops: workers take long lunch breaks since shopping is impossible at peak periods when they are supposed to get to or leave work. Another is accidents at work (see 10 below). Another, often alleged and to my mind plausible, is the death of Stalin and the end of the terror. For Stalin's terror was at least as much economic as political. Of declining idealism (which would clearly affect discipline adversely) we have not spoken these 45 years: that which has totally declined cannot be declining. The question is, can cynicism express itself openly? And the answer seems to be, in the reduced terror, yes. This leads very directly to—

8. Corruption, which comes in three forms.

(a) First is the benign plan violation, which makes official output possible. For instance the director buys some essential components on the black market in order that his plan may be fulfilled; or bribes another director to do something not strictly in his plan, for the same purpose. In these cases there is no extra black production, only a black redistribution of resources whose production has already been duly recorded as produced. But this type of redistribution is after all black: it has involved diversion of funds, breach of the law and the greasing of palms. It appears not to have widely increased since the planning problems which it solves are endemic; but the bribes paid appear to have risen a great deal.

(b) Other corruption arises from a genuine addition to output — black production, not officially recorded. The great cases are home-brewing ('samogon'), building repairs, meat, medical services and motor transport. Characteristically there is great reliance on inputs (grain, bricks, bread,[8] medicine, petrol) stolen from the state. However quickly this has grown it could hardly have affected overall figures of growth. The only estimate we have is a very dangerous one indeed: it added 9 per cent to net national product in 1965 (Wiles, 1979). If it was adding 18 per cent in 1980 (a not unreasonable figure, well below the Italian) this would add 0.53 per cent p.a. to the growth of the economy. But it would of course add 18 per cent to the level, and that is quite a respectable figure. For comparative purposes, however, all countries need additions of about that amount.

(c) Lastly there is private black market redistribution: the bribe the shop-assistant takes to hold something back for a favoured customer, the money you pay a pensioner to stand in a queue for you, or to a doctor to have your operation brought forward. None of this should count in statistical records of output, whether official or black.[9] To this kind of thing should be added bribes to policemen to let one off traffic offences, to passport officials, etc.

But it is extremely important not to be too economic about corruption. Whereas being corrupted is a tolerable feeling, corrupting is not – and many more people have to do the latter. A government under which corruption rises is an unpopular government, just as is one that presides over the rise in any crime. It is part of 'economic performance' in the wider sense that people be contented and honest in their economic dealings.

Again the addition to official output in (b) above has to be made for the completeness of the statistical record. It is not implied that this diversion of energies and stolen materials added to total actual output. On the contrary it subtracted, since the state sector is more efficient.[10] So the growth of (b) has been a negative factor.

9. Keeping people from work (7 above), killing them young (10 below), and fuelled by 'samogon' and theft (8 above), alcoholism deserves a special mention. This very old vice now grips perhaps 18 per cent of non-Moslem adult males and 9 per cent of such females, according to what Communist Party lecturers are telling the population.[11] 'Samogon' is about one quarter of all output (Wiles, 1980). The purely alcoholic breakfast is a very common sight. The southern Christian peoples of Moldavia and Transcaucasia, by tradition wine-bibbers, are succumbing to the more inebriating spirits of the Slavic north. The state has dared to put up prices again in 1981, but will it reduce output? For money wages will still buy more vodka than 20 years ago, and higher prices or lower outputs mean more 'samogon'.

Except for hashish, the Moslem's harmless alcohol, the modern drug scene has scarcely arrived. But Moslems are learning to drink, no doubt mainly during military service.

I do not consider myself obliged or competent to explain the spread of alcoholism. I observe only, and very banally, that people becoming addicted to alcohol are already unhappy.

10. No such paper as this should fail to mention the rising rates of age-specific mortality, perhaps the most surprising of all social

phenomena in this continually surprising country. In Table 7.2 I reproduce the data copied from Soviet statistical yearbooks by the US Bureau of the Census (1980) until their suppression after the appearance of the yearbook in 1977. Note that infantile mortality data were already suppressed in 1975. Broadly, *all* rates turned up in 1971, but the above-35s had enjoyed a brief plateau, beginning their upward journey in 1965 (the above-60s in 1961).

Is there anything like this in any other half-way developed country? Not in Britain, a country I have singled out as an economic disaster. But in the USA there is! Table 7.5 shows an increase in the age-specific mortality of white males, but not of other groups, between 1967 and 1977. In both years we notice another pathological phenomenon: a fall in these rates at the same moment of time between the ages of 22 and 28-9. The other groups are not affected, though white females come close to it: consider ages 23-4 in 1977.

Further evidence (Table 7.3) demonstrates that it is Soviet males that have most contributed to the Soviet results. The case is worse than in the USA, because the high excess mortality continues into much older age-groups. In the USA we learn that the ages principally affected are dying often of homicides, motor-vehicle accidents and suicides — the latter drug and drink-related (McCaslin, 1981; she makes no distinctions of sex and colour). The Russians publish no mortality or cause-of-death statistics, but Professor Urlanis, the very distinguished author of this table, elsewhere[12] attributes the excess of male mortality to smoking, drinking and accidents: which are the causes everywhere. Unfortunately we have no later breakdown by both age and sex; but it certainly looks as if in the 1960s the very gently increasing mortality had been the result of two opposing trends: increasing male self-destruction and medical progress. In the seventies alcoholism must have begun to make inroads among women too, for mentally retarded and monstrous babies are on the increase, or at any rate very numerous: 3 per cent of live births,[13] as opposed to 0.75 per cent in the UK. Female mortality must surely also have increased.

Can we learn anything about the USSR from the USA? Only, perhaps that males are more violent, more exposed to deadly machinery and more likely to take to drink than females. We are not even talking about the same age-groups, but at least we know that the phenomenon of rising age-specific mortality, in a more or less civilised country suffering neither famine nor war, is possible. It does not have to be statistical mirage. But a much more convincing example is Poland, also a Communist country with a traditional drink problem and a cold climate.

An identical effect, or series of effects, can be observed, starting about 1970: the male deterioration is much greater than the female deterioration, and all age groups between 20 and 60 are affected.[14]

Can the explanation be that generations weakened by traumatic experiences in their early youth are successively reaching 40+ and so dying off more rapidly now for reasons unconnected with current events? It seems, not so: in Table 7.4 we rearrange Table 7.2 to show that date of birth and traumatic early experiences have nothing to do with it. Simply, people born at later times, be they bad times (1916-20; 1931-5) or good ones (1921-30), die more at the same age.

So much remains to be explained. But what light does the increase in mortality throw on the Soviet economic situation? After all the rich can develop fatal consumption habits: the Roman rich used lead plumbing, and over-ate to the point of deliberate nausea; the white American boys who kill themselves can afford the expensive machines and drugs that are the instruments of their self-destruction. The Soviet male's undoubted increased purchasing power over vodka is a sign of increased wealth; and if some is left over for buying motor vehicles the combined result is drunken driving − and so more death.

This might indeed be part of the explanation for the rising mortality of the male aged 30-64; such increases as 3-9 in 10,000 could plausibly be laid to alcohol and machinery. But increases of 50 in 10,000 at or around birth cannot be so explained, and we are bound to look to such factors as increased poverty and increased medical inefficiency (also a sign of poverty).

Yet all this swims counter to what we (think we) know. Incomes have incontestably become more equal; the purchasing power of pensions, and above all the population's eligibility for them, have risen steeply (McAuley, 1979, passim). The rise in mortality sets in far too early (1966 for 60+, 1970 for infants) to sit comfortably with any speculation about economic failure to be valid. In particular, the government's per capita real expenditures on health, which are the vast majority of all health expenditures, seem to have risen consistently since 1965.[15]

Further to confuse us, the fertility rate, a sure indicator of morale over a short period, has not fallen since 1970. That is, children born to 1000 women of child-bearing age were 88.9 in 1959, 66.9 in 1970, 70.5 in 1979-80.[16]

Can, finally, these demographic trends have caused an economic downturn? Here the overwhelmingly important question is the actual dependency ratio, given the actual state of the age-pyramid at the starting date, not the effects of small changes in age-specific mortality. This ratio has moved from 52.5 per cent in 1929 through 52.3 per cent in 1973, to 48.5 per cent in 1979,[17] so there is no problem here: there are fewer children to look after, and pensioners have not quite filled their place.

The right answer is, surely, to treat the demographic trends as part of the decline of labour discipline: loose behaviour of one kind and another is on the increase, and before the occasional early death comes a great deal of early sickness and absenteeism.

11. What, finally, of the military burden? Spread as it is between consumption and investment, concealed behind the most suspicious of all the figures on the budget,[18] the military burden is hard to tease out. The CIA has made the most confidence-destroying revisions of its estimates, furthermore. But as usual the growth rate is more believable than the absolute US/Soviet comparison, which we do not need. A fairly recent estimate is that defence expenditures have grown at 2.9 per cent p.a. in 1970-9[19] with a slight deceleration in 1976 — say 3.0 per cent and then 2.6 per cent.

To these we must add, since January 1980, expenditures in Afghanistan. The costing of wars is a very undeveloped art. At least we have now detailed figures for the Falklands war, and can proceed by analogy. That war has cost £500 m. in equipment loss, and £500 m. in all else, in two and a half months ('The Times', 10 June 1982). Put, for Afghanistan, one twentieth as much equipment loss, but twice as much other expenditure (four times as many men engaged, but fewer missiles and more bullets). We arrive at £5 bn. annually or, at the high military purchasing power parity of the rouble, R. 5 bn. This is 0.9 per cent of GNP, and it must surely have been added to the planned defence burden. As the insurgents get better arms, this figure will rise. Military foreign aid is included in the defence figure. Military deliveries to the Third World have risen five-fold since the late sixties, and may have been about $3,700 million per annum in 1978 (ed. Wiles, 1982, p. 375), or 0.3 per cent of GNP. This includes, sales for cash, which must of course be netted out of the defence burden, and are probably very profitable.

It is also fair to mention foreign civilian aid in this section. In 1978 this was running, in hard terms of actual deliveries less debt amortisation, also at about $3,700 million per annum (ed. Wiles, 1982, p. 42). This figure includes aid within CMEA. In 1981 Poland and Afghanistan were unexpectedly expensive, and they will be more so in 1982. But other items could be cut, notably Cuba.

On balance it is clear that defence plus foreign aid will outgrow a very stagnant national product, and be a bigger burden. But until recently they hardly did. The size of the burden has however nearly always been big: about 13 per cent of GNP[20] since at least 1970.

12. How can we dare to sum this up? We have pointed to a few hard causes of the recent downturn:

(a) the efficiency of labour is being lowered by intensifying alcoholism (section 9).

(b) it also suffers from the depressing effect of and diversion of energy by queues. These are themselves normally due not to shortages as understood by the man in the street, but to accumulating liquidity and stable prices (section 3).

(c) the lowered profitability of imported technology indicates the approach of true 'advanced status' in many fields with the slower growth that this implies

(d) there are sharply diminishing returns to activities based on natural resources (section 6).

(e) Everyone has underestimated the extra drain of the Afghan war (section 11).

We have suggested too a general spiritual malaise, lying behind the alcoholism and also directly affecting the efficiency of labour (section 6).

These items apart, we look in vain for some new flaw in the system to be causing the deterioration in its performance. Nor have the effects of any of the above points been quantified. Econometricians have tried (12c) and failed.[21] The attempt to quantify (12d) is in its infancy. There will never be a statistical base from which to attack the others. We do not know very much.

Notes

1. It is of great importance that by quite different reasoning the Wharton Institute has arrived at the same conclusion: compare the figures for Soviet consumpion in Daniel Bond's contribution to the next NATO annual (Brussels, late 1982). It was a great pleasure, furthermore, to find Ellman giving the same answer here — the opportunity to make last minute corrections was sternly rejected! Information also reaches me, via a single intermediary, that a senior Soviet academician of international standing takes the same view. The same view is taken by a less distinguished Soviet economist who visited Birmingham recently.

2. As we call the purely accounting money with which one enterprise pays another. Since outputs are produced and inputs acquired according to the quantitative command plan, it does not matter much what prices are in passive money.

3. My own workings, partly based on private Soviet information. Cf. however Wiles in 'Die Parallelwirtschaft' (Bundesinstitut für Ostwissenschaftliche Studien, Cologne, 1979), pp. 115–16; Eugene Zaleski, 'Stalinist Planning . . .' (North Carolina, 1980), p. 441; Raymond Powell in Vladimir G. Treml and John P.

Hardt (eds.), 'Soviet Economic Statistics' (North Carolina, 1972), pp. 404–6;
Igor Birman, 'Secret Incomes of the Soviet State Budget' (The Hague, 1981),
pp. 119, 128.

4. From official sources except for Hungarian cash – Wiles in 'Economie
Appliquée' (January 1974), p. 139.

5. This very oversimplified version elides many qualifications: the differences
between housewives and other people; the reason why we continue to work
42 hours – it's in the contract; the possibilities of early retirement, prolonged
schooling and simple unemployment. None of them detracts from the essential
rightness of our picture of the queue.

6. In private conversation. On all this cf. Philip Hanson, 'Trade and Techno-
logy in Soviet-Western Relations' (New York, 1981); ibid., A Backlash against
Technology Imports? (Radio Free Europe – Radio Liberty, Munich, 12
November 1981).

7. In 'Finansy SSSR', (December 1981), p. 4.

8. Black meat output is mostly urban: pigs are fed the super-cheap bread
since fodder is expensive.

9. Though it may have made it possible. Thus if the doctor had stood in the
queue he would have performed no operations at all.

10. Though not at building repairs and tailoring.

11. i.e. there were 22 m. 'alcoholics' (whatever that means) in the country in
1980, David Willis in 'Christian Science Monitor' (2 February 1981). There were
c. 76 m. men and c. 91.1 m. women aged 18 or over of non-Moslem
nationality. I have arbitrarily assigned the 22 m. among the sexes so that the male
ratio is double the female.

12. B.Ts. Urlanis, 'Dinamika i Struktura Naseleniya SSSR i SShA' (Moscow,
1964), p. 115.

13. 'Sovetski Meditsin' (November 1981). The reader is warned that these
terms are dangerously undefined.

14. 'Rocznik Statystyczny', 'Rocznik Demograficzny', various issues.

15. Workings (which are quite crude) available on request. The same result
emerges from the unexplained workings of Gertrude Schroeder and Barbara
Severin up to 1975, in 'Soviet Economy in a New Perspective' (Joint Economic
Committee of the US Congress, Washington, 1976), p. 759.

16. Census 1970, vol. II, pp. 12–13; 'Vestnik Statistiki' (November 1981), p. 71.

17. Population not employed in state or co-operative sectors: Nar.Khoz.
1979, p. 9. When we consider that the private economy, legal and illegal together,
has much increased in this period, this change is an underestimate.

18. Alone among budgetary expenditures and revenues, military expenditure
estimates have always been exactly fulfilled since 1963 inclusive! They are also
about two-fifths as big as the CIA's rouble estimate.

19. Measured, alas, from a bar graph – CIA (1980), p. 4. There are many
definitional problems, of course.

20. This is from the reportage in 'Businessweek' (28 February 1977), which is
an excellent entrée into this arcane subject. 13 per cent is the CIA's figure just
after their great revision, referred to in the text.

21. Cf. Stanislaw Gomulka and Alec Nove, 'The Econometrical Evaluation
of Technology Transfer' (OECD, Paris, 1982).

References

Giffen, J., 1981, The Allocation of Investment in the Soviet Union, 'Soviet Studies', October

Hanson, P., 1981, Economic Constraints on Soviet Policies in the 1980s, 'International Affairs', vol. 57, winter 1980/1

McAuley, A., 1979, 'Economic Welfare in the Soviet Union', George Allen & Unwin, London

McCaslin, 1981, Letter to the 'New York Times'

Wiles, P., 1979, 'Die Parallelwirtschaft', Bundesinstitut für Ostwissenschaftliche Studien, Cologne

Wiles, P., 1982, Soviet Consumption and Investment Crisis, 'Soviet Studies', April

Wiles, P., 1982, A Note on the Cost of Soviet Oil, NATO, Economic Directorate CMEA, 'Energy 1980-1990', Brussels

Wiles, P. (ed.), 1982, 'The New Communist Third World', Croom Helm, London and Canberra

Table 7.1: Soviet Economic Growth, 1951–81 (per cent per annum)

	1951–5	1956–60	1961–5	1966–70	1971–5	1976–8	1979	1980	1981
A. National Income									
1a. Soviet official (national income produced)	11.4	9.1	6.5	7.7	5.7	5.1	2.6	3.4	
1b. (1a) corrected (Wiles)						2.1	0.8	1.1	
1c. Soviet official (national income utilised)						4.2	1.8	4.3	3.2
2. GNP (Greenslade-CIA)	6.0	5.8	5.0	7.1	5.1	3.6	1.2	0.8	
3. Population (Soviet official)	1.9	1.8	1.5	1.0	0.9	0.8	0.9		
B. Industry									
4. Soviet official (global output)	13.1	10.4	8.6	8.5	7.4	5.1	3.4	3.3	3.4
5. Greenslade-CIA (net output)	11.3	8.7	7.0	6.8	6.0	3.9	2.3		
6. Factor inputs	7.4	5.3	6.4	5.5	4.8	4.6			
C. Agriculture									
7. Soviet official (global output)	6.1	4.9	3.4	3.3	2.1	4.5			
8. Diamond & Davis CIA (net outputs)	4.8	4.7	2.9	3.1	1.6		1.2	−4.0	
9. Factor inputs	3.3	2.0	2.8	1.3	2.0				−2.0

Sources: Generally I owe this table to Hanson, 1981 (Table 1).

Row

1b. See text above. The source is Wiles in Soviet Studies, 1982.

1a. and 1c. 'Nar. Khoz.', 1974, p. 53; 'Nar. Khoz.', 1978, p. 43; 'USSR in Figures for 1980', p. 26; 'Pravda', 24 January 1982.

2. To 1970: R. Greenslade, The Real Gross National Product of the USSR; 1970–75, US Congress Joint Economic Committee, 'Soviet Economy in a New Perspective', Washington; Government Printing ER 78-10512, 'The Soviet Economy in 1976–77 and Outlook for 1978', Washington: CIA, 1978, p. 1. 1976–78: Idem, Handbook of Economic Statistics 1979, Washington: CIA, 1979, p. 26.

4. As for 1a. and 1c.

5. To 1975: Greenslade, The Real Gross National Product of the USSR. From 1975: NFAC, 'Handbook of Economic Statistics 1979', p. 65.

6. F.D. Whitehouse and R. Converse, Soviet Industry (source as in 8) vol. I p. 414; Greenslade as in (2).

7. See 1a. and 1c. These are five-year averages: thus '1956–60' is the average for 1958–62, divided by that for 1965–7. For 1976–9 I used a three year average, 1978–80 and a five year average 1972–7.

8. D.B. Diamond and W.L. Davis, Comparative Growth in Output and Productivity in the US, and USSR Agriculture in 'Soviet Economy in a Time of Change', US Congress Joint Economic Committee, Washington, US GPO 1979, vol. II, pp. 49–50.

9. As in (8). See (6). The inputs are labour, land, capital, current industrial inputs and productive livestock, as weighted by Mr. Diamond.

Table 7.2: Reported and Estimated Age-specific Death Rates in the USSR: 1958 to 1976[a] (compilation by the US Bureau of the Census, 1980, p. 2)

Age group	1958–9	1969–60	1960–1	1961–2	1962–3	1963–4	1964–5	1965–6	1966–7
All ages	7.4	7.3	7.2	7.4	7.4	7.1	7.1	7.3	7.5
0–1	40.6	35.3	32.3	32.2	30.9	28.8	27.2	26.1	26.0
0–4	11.9	NA	9.9	NA	8.7	7.8	7.2	6.9	6.9
5–9	1.1	NA	1.0	NA	0.9	0.8	0.8	0.8	0.8
10–14	0.8	NA	0.7	NA	0.7	0.6	0.6	0.6	0.6
15–19	1.3	NA	1.2	NA	1.1	1.0	1.0	1.0	1.0
20–4	1.8	NA	1.7	NA	1.6	1.6	1.6	1.6	1.5
25–9	2.2	NA	2.1	NA	2.0	2.0	2.0	2.0	2.0
30–4	2.6	NA	2.7	NA	2.6	2.5	2.5	2.6	2.6
35–9	3.1	NA	3.0	NA	3.1	3.1	3.1	3.2	3.4
40–4	4.0	NA	3.7	NA	3.8	3.7	3.8	3.9	4.1
45–9	5.4	NA	5.4	NA	5.3	5.1	5.0	5.1	5.3
50–4	7.9	NA	7.5	NA	7.7	7.7	7.8	7.9	7.9
55–9	11.2	NA	10.9	NA	11.2	10.7	10.8	11.1	11.3
60–4	17.1	NA	16.7	NA	17.5	17.1	17.2	17.2	17.4
65–9	25.2	NA	24.6	NA	25.6	24.1	24.4	25.5	25.9
70 and over	63.8	NA	63.0	NA	67.7	63.6	64.2	65.8	66.1

Table 7.2 (contd.)

Age group	1967-8	1968-9	1969-70	1970-1	1971-2	1972-3	1973-4	1974-5	1975-6
All ages	7.7	7.9	8.2	8.2	8.4	8.6	8.7	9.0	9.4
0-1	26.4	25.8	24.7	22.9	24.7	26.4	27.9	29.4[b]	31.1[b]
0-4	7.0	7.0	6.9	6.7	6.8	7.2	7.7	8.2	8.7
5-9	0.7	0.7	0.7	0.7	0.7	0.7	0.7	0.7	0.7
10-14	0.6	0.6	0.6	0.5	0.5	0.5	0.5	0.5	0.5
15-19	1.0	1.0	1.0	1.0	1.0	1.0	1.0	1.0	1.0
20-4	1.5	1.5	1.6	1.6	1.6	1.6	1.6	1.7	1.7
25-9	2.1	2.2	2.2	2.2	2.1	2.1	2.0	2.1	2.1
30-4	2.7	2.8	2.8	2.8	2.8	2.8	2.8	3.0	3.0
35-9	3.5	3.5	3.7	3.8	3.7	3.6	3.6	3.7	3.8
40-4	4.3	4.6	4.7	4.7	4.8	4.8	4.9	5.2	5.3
45-9	5.5	5.6	6.0	6.0	6.1	6.2	6.4	6.7	6.9
50-4	8.0	8.1	8.7	8.7	8.8	8.6	8.8	9.0	9.3
55-9	11.5	12.1	11.7	11.8	11.9	12.5	12.3	13.0	13.4
60-4	17.8	18.2	18.0	17.9	18.1	18.0	18.2	18.3	18.9
65-9	26.3	27.5	27.5	26.9	26.8	27.2	27.0	27.4	28.0
70 and over	66.8	67.3[c]	75.7[c]	74.9	74.8	75.5	73.5	73.3	75.0

Notes: NA Not available.

a. The infant mortality rate, shown in row '0-1', is a yearly one. The first entry is for 1959. All other rates are two-year moving averages of yearly rates, which express the number of deaths per 1000 in a given age group.

b. Estimated [sc. by the Bureau of the Census].

c. A remarkably large increase took place in the death rates of persons 70 years of age and older between 1968-9 and 1969-70. It is not known why only these two age groups were affected, whether, or example, a statistical change took place or better coverage was initiated before the 1970 census.

Table 7.3: Urlanis' Sex- and Age-mortality Rates, USSR

	1958–9 (%)		1969–70 (%)		M/F (5%)	
	M	F	M	F	1958–9	1969–70
15–19	1.5	0.9	1.5	0.6	170	250
20–4	2.4	1.3	2.3	0.8	186	287
25–9	3.0	1.5	3.4	1.1	202	309
30–4	3.5	1.7	4.3	1.4	207	307
35–9	4.4	2.2	5.6	1.9	202	294
40–4	5.9	2.9	7.1	2.6	202	273
45–9	7.9	3.8	9.4	3.8	209	247
50–4	12.0	5.5	13.7	5.7	219	240
55–9			18.8	7.7		
60–4			28.1	12.5		
65–9			41.2	21.1		

Source: B.Ts. Urlanis, 'Problemy Dinamiki Naseleniya SSSR' (Moscow, 1974), pp. 186–91.

Table 7.3: Table 7.2 Re-arranged: Mortality by Birth Year

Year born	Age	25–9	30–4	35–9	40–4	45–9	50–4	55–9	60–4	65–9	(Year in general time)
1936–40		2.0	2.8	3.8							
1931–5		2.1	2.6	3.8	5.3						
1926–30			2.7a	3.2	4.7	6.9					
1921–5				3.0	3.9	6.0	9.3				
1916–20					3.7	5.1	8.7	13.4			
1911–15						5.4a	7.9	11.8	18.9		
1906–10							7.5	11.1	17.9	28.0	
1901–9								10.9	17.2	26.9	(75/6)
1896–1900									16.7	25.5	(70/1)
1891–5										24.6	(65/6)
											(60/1)

Note. a. These figures are the sole exceptions to the generalisation in the text.
By reading diagonally we rediscover the age-specific mortality rates at a given year in general time as given in Table 7.2.

Table 7.5: Mortality Rate per Thousand USA

Age	1967 White Male	1967 White Female	1967 Black & other Male	1967 Black & other Female	1977 White Male	1977 White Female	1977 Black & other Male	1977 Black & other Female	White M/F (%) 1967	White M/F (%) 1977
14	0.80	0.37	1.02	0.51	0.77	0.35	0.80	0.38	216	220
15	1.03	0.44	1.29	0.60	1.05	0.44	1.00	0.46	234	239
16	1.26	0.52	1.58	0.70	1.32	0.52	1.21	0.55	242	254
17	1.45				1.53	0.58				275
18	1.59	normal	normal	normal	1.68	0.61	normal	normal		
19	1.68				1.76	0.60				
20	1.77	0.61	2.80	1.12	1.84	0.60	2.25	0.85	290	307
21	1.85				1.92	0.60				325
22	1.88	normal	normal	normal	1.95	0.60	normal	normal		
23	1.86				1.93	0.60				
24	1.79				1.86	0.59				
25	1.70	0.65	3.87	1.61	1.79	0.59	3.51	1.20	262	303
26	1.62				1.71	0.59				275
27	1.57	normal	normal	normal	1.65	0.60	normal	normal		
28	1.56				1.61	0.62				
29	1.59	0.76	4.62	2.28	1.59	0.65	3.97	1.42	209	245
30	1.63	0.81	4.87	2.54	1.58	0.69	3.95	1.47	201	229
31	1.68	0.86	5.13	2.80	1.59	0.73	3.96	1.53	195	218

Note. 'Normal' means pursuing an upward course with age and a downward course with time.
Annual Abstract (1970), p. 54. Statistical Abstract (1979), p. 71.

8 SOVIET ECONOMIC PERFORMANCE: A COMMENT ON WILES AND ELLMAN

Alec Nove

The slowdown in Soviet growth is denied by no one. Nor are the serious shortages and imbalances that plague the economy. Indeed, both Wiles and Ellman raise the interesting question of the degree of exaggeration built into the official growth indices, suggesting that slow growth may actually be no growth at all. Before discussing causes, let me dwell on this very important question.

The tendency to understate price increases (or overstate price reductions, eg. in machinery), and therefore to overstate the rate of growth by using an incorrect deflator, has been commented on by many writers. Thus I devoted pp. 361-3 of my 'Soviet economic system' to this question, and presented and interpreted some data published in 'Voprosy ekonomiki' (by Krasovsky and Fal'tsman) in articles in 'Soviet Studies' (January and April 1981). In another article not yet published, I draw attention to the data presented by Lokshin about retail prices ('Voprosy ekonomiki', No. 10, 1981) which show that in most instances in which we have data on the value per unit sold and the official price index for the given item, the former is far above the latter. To cite but one example, the average price for footwear rose by 33 per cent in the period 1970–80, while the price index for footwear stands at 99.5 ('Nar. Khoz.', 1980, p. 439).

However, it is one thing to have a well-based view concerning the existence of exaggeration (of growth) or understatement (of price increases), but quite another to attempt quantification. Let me briefly define the nature of the problem.

In all countries, when models alter, new products are introduced, old products vanish, the price and volume indices are imperfect approximations. Economists and statisticians talk of 'hedonic indices', which fully reflect altered quality characteristics, and remind us that the changing patterns of demand are relevant too, so that we should ideally need to know about the customers' indifference curves: does the 'new' assortment conform to their preferences? Of course in the real world we do not have all this information, and a 'hedonic' index presents awkward conceptual problems: thus if product A has ten quality characteristics, what weights should be attached to each, and why?

This is not to argue that Soviet indices are no 'worse' than ours. It is important, however, never to lose sight of the fact that it is because comparisons of unlike with unlike are of their nature imprecise that the Soviet statistics can be distorted without there being any outright cheating or falsification. The key elements which differentiate their figures from ours are, in my view, the following:

a. There is a sellers' market; the customer can usually be made to buy whatever is available.

b. Where the customer is another enterprise, there is no disincentive to purchase dearer inputs. On the contrary, until now, the dearer the better, so long as they can be included in costings for price-fixing. The construction industry's plan targets have been the money they spend, so they positively welcome dearer inputs, as many Soviet sources testify.

c. The selling enterprise is interested in high gross sales figures (or 'val'), and benefits from a shift towards dearer products old and new.

d. Price control over old products is best evaded by introducing new ones, or 'new' ones, of allegedly better quality.

The recent attempts to devise 'normed value added' indicators are irrelevant in the present context, as this does not affect the figures up to 1981.

In the West the firms are interested primarily in profits, and hardly at all in growth statistics or what the central statisticians do to devise a price index. There is no price control to evade.

Let us then agree that all this must cause the statistics to be wrong, and particularly so where changes in model or design are frequent. How can this be quantified?

Let us first take a consumers' good: footwear. As shown above, the average price of shoes has gone up. Probably, or possibly, so has quality. Possibly, demand has shifted towards dearer shoes. On the evidence before us, how can we say what the 'real' price increase has been? If citizens seek the cheap shoes in vain, and have no choice but to buy the dearer ones, that is a different ball game than one where they leave the cheap shoes on the counter and line up for the dearer 'real leather' ones. For some products, the unit values are plainly unusable: thus the average price of television sets has risen but the price index (so it is claimed) has fallen. In this case the claim could be correct, since there has been a big rise in the share of the much dearer colour sets, which are apparently in heavy demand.

Or let us move on to machinery. Krasovsky's evidence (cited in my article) strongly supports the view that the official price index is faulty, i.e. that many machines are much dearer than the ones they replace, and/or that the improvement in their productivity is not proportional to the extra cost, and also that construction costs rise in ostensibly 'unchanged prices'. Fal'tsman gives some data about the rising cost of investment required to produce a given quantity of output, what he calls 'moshchnostnyi ekvivalent', 'capacity equivalent'. Wiles seems to suggest that these and other published critical comments enable us to calculate the 'real' price and/or volume indices. Surely this is not so, because some factors other than prices influence investment costs: these could include additional costs of environmental protection, less favourable natural conditions (e.g. in the extractive industries), and so on. Also the information that the investments required to produce a ton of steel have risen by (say) 5 per cent per annum tell us nothing about their effects on labour productivity or quality. It should also be borne in mind that any index purporting to represent the whole category 'machinery and metal-working' includes within it a sizeable volume of consumer durables and a large amount of military hardware, neither of these being 'machinery' of the kind involved in investments. Krasovsky specifically deplored the absence of a price index for investment as such. (Incidentally, do we publish or calculate such an index?)

All this is not intended to cast doubt on the facts that price and volume indices respectively understate and overstate what they purport to represent. Nor is it intended to cast any aspersions on many attempts — eg. by Becker, Schroeder, Greenslade, the CIA — to try to calculate what has really happened to prices. Certainly I do not pretend to be able to do better. I would agree — indeed I have argued this in print — that the prices and costs of investment have recently been rising faster than the so-called 'volume' of investment in so-called unchanged prices, and that therefore the real volume of investment may have fallen, this constituting one important reason for the decline in growth rates. It is reasonable to put forward the hypothesis that if the official industrial growth index falls to 3 per cent or so, the disguised and not precisely measurable price inflation is likely to reduce this in 'real' terms to a mere 1 per cent or even close to zero. However, it must be recalled that these distortions operate unevenly in different sectors. Thus agricultural output is unaffected, and so is energy or most kinds of industrial materials and semi-manufactures.

Wiles quite correctly refers to increased shortages as a negative factor. More queueing, less choice, more absenteeism, less discipline. Shortages of producers' goods and building labour contribute to long gestation periods for investment, which also contributes to lower growth rates.

I doubt if Wiles is right in ascribing slowdown to having caught up with Western technology: the evidence suggests vast unutilised opportunities for improvement: lack of 'small-scale mechanisation', obsolete equipment in non-priority industries, exceptionally wasteful utilisation of existing machinery (on this last point see the devastating pair of articles by Kheinman in 'EKO', Nos. 5 and 6, 1980). Wiles also has an odd statement (p. 149) which suggests that the very large share of agriculture in total investment does not 'differ from any capitalist country'. Surely not so. Is it not much higher in the USSR than in any capitalist country?

Wiles's estimates of 'black' output may be correct, but he would probably agree that they are necessarily very rough, especially if one seeks to measure their change through time. Meat appears rather surprisingly on his list of black output. Why? Pigs may be privately owned, meat can be legally sold. True, pigs may not be kept in cities (as distinct from their outer suburbs), but that is true also in London and Glasgow, and how can a pig be concealed from prying eyes? According to Shmelev ('Voprosy ekonomiki', No. 5, 1981, p. 68) the share of 'workers and employees' in output of private plots is around 50 per cent; private plots are in the hands of 13 million kolkhoz peasants, 10 million state-farm families and about 10 million workers and employees of other spheres of the economy. Of course not all of them keep animals, but many millions clearly do so. What is true is that there are considerable unregistered and unrecorded sales of farm produce, additional to those in the markets, and reference is made to this by Shmelev in this same article (p. 70). The spread of private motoring has led (inter alia) to townsmen going to villages to buy produce directly from peasants. But this does not mean that the production is unrecorded, or that the transaction is 'black'.

Alcoholism must be a contributory factor to the rise in death rate, to which Wiles very properly refers. He mentions briefly the military burden, and I suspect that he understates the impact on growth of the diversion of so much of the best brains and technology into the totally unproductive defence sector. Several of my 'eastern' colleagues, in informal conversations, have mentioned this as the first on the list of causes of economic strain. I would add one other factor: the increasing inability of the central planners to coordinate a very large and complex economy, due partly to its sheer size and partly to what Brezhnev calls 'vedomstvennost' and 'mestnichestvo', departmentalism and localism, which could be seen as the indiscipline of middle-grade officialdom, the lack of power (and information) at the centre to ensure coherence of plans and their execution, which leads to more imbalances and bottlenecks, which have cumulative effects. Steel and coal output in 1981 were both significantly below 1978 levels in absolute terms, quite contrary to plan. Railway bottlenecks have become much more serious. And so on.

Turning now to Ellman's contribution, he too is properly sceptical about the official price index — though 'statistical trickery' is a harsh way of describing the phenomenon we have been analysing. Also it is easy to calculate what has happened to prices in the collective-farm markers, though no figures give them explicitly: every 'Nar.khoz.' gives market turnover in actual prices and in state retail prices, and an index can be derived by dividing one into the other; this shows a clearly rising trend. I take this to be the source of the evidence which Ellman cites from Severin, and which I have also presented several times (e.g. 'Political economy and Soviet socialism', p. 185). I do not follow his argument about the national income data for 1980. There may indeed be a bigger-than-usual difference between the official and the 'real' price index, for the reasons given by Ellman. But surely not a bigger-than-usual difference between the rise in national income in current and in ('official') unchanged prices. Ellman's points on shortages and their direct and indirect effects are well taken. We should all pay more attention to the effects of unavailability on the standard of living and on the meaning of price quotations: even if prices were nominally unaltered, the disappearance of goods from the shops at those prices is a matter which surely affects real purchasing power, though in a manner difficult to quantify.

Ellman's table 2 is a surprising example of 'roman à thèse' statistics! Fast-growing items, such as gas, are simply omitted, and three of the items are directly or indirectly the consequence of three bad grain harvests in a row. The facts are gloomy enough without such a selective presentation. The general conclusions about relative stagnation are certainly correct, and must be causing acute concern to the Soviet leadership.

What remedies are being sought? Will they in fact succeed? It is worth examining the reforms introduced in the period 1979–81 from this point of view.

But first, let us define one extremely important aspect of the disease. I suggest that this can be subsumed under the heading of *diseconomies of scale*. The logic of the system requires the centre to acquire and digest information, and then to issue detailed binding orders, on a scale that is utterly impossible even to contemplate. True,

planning techniques have been improving, but the problems of operationally controlling a large and complex economy have been increasing
faster than the means available to cope with them. In a real sense the
system is both too centralised and not centralised enough: it requires a
degree of authority and control which it does not and cannot possess.
Thus one reason for the slow diffusion of technology is that technical
progress is not a matter which lends itself to central plan instructions
An order to produce a thousand tons of (say) sulphuric acid is much
more meaningful than an order to introduce a thousand innovations!
Nor has the centre the detailed knowledge to issue operational orders
to ensure that the machinery that is produced conforms to the requirements of the users, is economical and efficient, this being one example
among many of the lack of influence of the customer on production,
the neglect of use-value. Since prices are usually passive, use-value is
supposed to be incorporated (be reflected in) plan-instructions, but the
centre, to try to carry out its micro-economic duties, is compelled to
aggregate, to issue global plan-orders in tons, square metres, millions
of roubles or whatever, with consequences which are familiar. The
vastly complex task of matching supply with production plans is never
carried out satisfactorily, giving rise to the equally familiar phenomena
of 'self-supply', cross-hauls, hoarding, over-application for inputs, con-
cealment of potential, failure to get materials or machines of the
required specification, etc. The scale of the planning operation compels
its division between different units: ministries, state committees,
localities, etc. These develop their own vested interests, and the task of
coordinating them overwhelms the organs charged with these tasks.
(It may even drive them to drink, thereby contributing to alcoholism!)
One cause of the present troubles of the Soviet economy is that this
centralised system is increasingly unable to cope with the problems of
a modern industrial society at a time when reserves of labour are exhausted and growth depends decisively on productivity. Of course none
of these weaknesses or problems is new, but it is reasonable to see
them as becoming more acute through time.

Seen in this light, few of the reforms which have been promulgated
can make any significant difference, and some may actually make
things worse. In fact the only unambiguously positive set of measures
relates to the encouragement of the private sector in agriculture.
Virtually all the others have as one of their effects an increase in the
tasks of the central planners, overloading still further the impossibly
overloaded mechanism. Thus the 'normed value added' indicator is
predictably causing acute headaches: it requires calculations in respect

of millions of products, and the effect is bound to include anomalies: enterprises will find large gaps between their actual wages bill and profits and those which are 'normed', and will manoeuvre accordingly. This same decree of July 1979 includes a number of other compulsory indicators: volume of output 'of the most important products' in quantity, total value of sales, the fulfilment of planned delivery contracts, limits on the labour force, normed wage payments per unit of output (differentiated, presumably, by enterprises), cost reduction, etc. Inconsistencies are certain. To make matters worse, there is the decree published in 'Pravda' on 4 July 1981. Designed to achieve a (doubtless essential) economy in the use of energy and materials, it seeks to do so by methods which are bound to be counterproductive. Let me quote a key sentence from the decree: 'It is considered necessary to lay down in quinquennial and annual plans, for industrial, construction and transport ministries, associations and enterprises, beginning in 1983, tasks ('zadaniya') for costs of production . . ., and within these tasks, the limit (maximum level) of material expenditures in monetary terms per rouble of output'. There are to be revised and tighter norms for use of materials and energy, expressed in physical units, which are to be imposed on ministries and on republics, which these will then pass down to enterprise level. The list of material resources in respect of which the centre imposes norms of utilisation and targets for 'reducing utilisation norms' is to be increased. (The decree ends with decisions to publish a pamphlet on economy of materials and the design of posters to the same end.)

Surely all this cannot have a positive result. The multiplicity of indicators, their mutual inconsistency, their inevitable lack of connection with quality and with user requirements, will all stand in the way of a necessary and much-desired concentration on efficiency and on 'final results' (as against the fulfilment of quantitative or value targets for intermediate goods and services). The reform in prices now in progress is irrelevant, in so far as this is based on traditional principles, i.e. on cost-plus, with little or no attention paid to scarcity or to use-value. Hungary-type reforms, which might relieve the impossible pressure on the centre, have been considered and — so far — rejected. The worsening international climate, the economic consequences of the arms race, will scarcely incline the gerontocracy towards experiment. So one might expect stagnation to continue, and the political ill-effects of shortages and disappointed expectations might be mitigated by appeals to patriotism in the face of open American hostility. A new leadership might lay greater stress on discipline, the struggle against corruption, and aim for lesser dependence on the West, in view of the vulnerability of the economy to possible embargos. But prospects do not look encouraging, though it is not to be excluded that a still-unknown claimant to the leadership might find it pays politically to advocate radical changes in the increasingly obsolete system of centralised economic planning.

NOTES ON CONTRIBUTORS

STEPHEN BARKER graduated from Cambridge University in 1977 and is currently employed in the Ministry of Defence as a Senior Research Officer. For the past four years he has been engaged in economic research on Eastern Europe.

JAN DREWNOWSKI is a retired Professor of Economics. He was educated and gained his Dr Econ. Sc. at the Central School of Commerce (later re-named Central School of Planning and Statistics), Warsaw. He did postgraduate work at the London School of Economics from 1933 to 1935. He has held chairs of economics and/or planning at the School of Planning and Statistics (until 1961) and then at the University of Ghana and the Institute of Social Studies in the Hague. In 1946-8 and in 1956-61 he took active part in national economic planning in Poland. He has written in Polish and in English on economic theory, economics of socialism, the politics and economics of Poland and on economic and social problems of development.

MICHAEL ELLMAN is Professor of Economics at the University of Amsterdam. He studied at the universities of Cambridge, London and Moscow and has taught at the universities of Glasgow and Cambridge. His books include 'Soviet Planning Today' (1971), 'Planning Problems in the USSR' (1973) and 'Socialist Planning' (1979). He has published articles in the 'Economic Journal', 'Economica', 'Slavic Review', 'Critique', 'Soviet Studies', 'Cambridge Journal of Economics', 'Economics of Planning', 'Journal of Development Studies', 'World Development' and others. His main interests are in planning techniques and the political economy of socialism. In addition to his regular lectures at Amsterdam University, he has recently lectured in Copenhagen, Antwerp, Shanghai, Beijing, Amherst Mass., New York and Mexico City.

STANISLAW GOMULKA is a Senior Lecturer at the London School of Economics. He did his PhD thesis at Warsaw University, under Michal Kalecki and Oskar Lange, in 1966. He has lived in the West since 1969, mainly at the London School of Economics. In 1980/1 he became a Fellow of the Netherlands Institute for Advanced Studies. Most of his numerous publications are in the fields of economic growth and innovation, especially in reference to centrally planned economies.

ALEC NOVE was born in Petrograd and graduated at the London School of Economics in 1936. He served in the British Army from 1939 to 1946 and was a civil servant until 1958, when he was appointed Reader in Russian Social and Economic Studies at the London School of Economics. He has been Professor of Economics in Glasgow since 1963 and was also Director of the Institute of Soviet and East European Studies from 1963 to 1980. His publications include 'The Soviet Economic System', 'Economic History of the USSR', 'Stalinism and After' and 'Political Economy and Soviet Socialism'. He is a Fellow of the British Academy and the Royal Society of Edinburgh.

DOMENICO MARIO NUTI has been Professor of Political Economy and Director of the Centre for Russian and East European Studies at the University of Birmingham since 1980. He gained his 'Dottore in Giurisprudenza' in Rome in 1962, and his PhD in Economics at Cambridge in 1970. He was formerly Fellow of King's College Cambridge (1966-79) and lecturer at the Faculty of Economics and Politics, Cambridge University. He is the author of numerous publications on East European economies, with special reference to Poland.

ALAN SMITH is lecturer in the Economics of Eastern Europe at the School of Slavonic and East European Studies, University of London. He has been a visiting lecturer and Professor of Economics at Dartmouth College, Hanover, New Hampshire on three occasions. His publications include articles on the Romanian Economy, Comecon and Soviet and East European Economic Relations. He has contributed to the 'New Communist Third World' and is currently writing a book to be entitled 'The Planned Economies of Eastern Europe'.

PETER WILES is Professor of Russian Social and Economics Studies at the University of London. He was educated at New College, Oxford. His publications include: 'Price, Cost and Output', 'The Political Economy of Communism' and 'Communist International Economies'.

INDEX